QUEERSTORY

LGBTQ+

In common use since the 1990s, LGBTQ+ is the root of an ever-evolving acronym that aims to encompass and embrace the wide spectrum of nonheterosexual and noncisgender people in the world, and the movements that have organized to fight for their rights.

In order to avoid confusion, the acronym has been used as an umbrella term throughout this book. This may mean that LGBTQ+ sometimes retrospectively includes groups that would not have used the term to describe themselves. The word "queer" has been used as an inclusive term to describe a varied and extensive history of LGBTQ+ communities and culture across the twentieth and twenty-first centuries.

ABOUT LINDA RILEY
A Stonewall award winner and Icon of the Year in 2018, Linda Riley has dedicated her career to promoting and protecting LGBTQ+ rights. She is a former director of US LGBTQ+ campaign group GLAAD and adviser to the British Labour Party on diversity issues. She is the current publisher of the iconic DIVA, Europe's leading magazine for LGBTQ+ women, as well as the founder of the Rainbow Honours and the European and British Diversity awards.

QUEERSTORY

An Infographic History of the Fight for LGBTQ+ Rights

Foreword by Linda Riley

TILLER PRESS

New York London Toronto Sydney New Delhi

CONTENTS

1 Before Stonewall

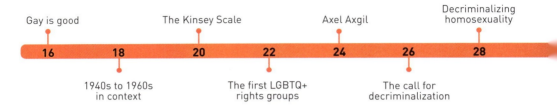

- 16 Gay is good
- 18 1940s to 1960s in context
- 20 The Kinsey Scale
- 22 The first LGBTQ+ rights groups
- 24 Axel Axgil
- 26 The call for decriminalization
- 28 Decriminalizing homosexuality

2 LGBTQ+ Liberation

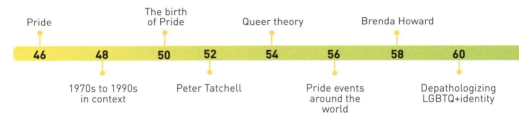

- 46 Pride
- 48 1970s to 1990s in context
- 50 The birth of Pride
- 52 Peter Tatchell
- 54 Queer theory
- 56 Pride events around the world
- 58 Brenda Howard
- 60 Depathologizing LGBTQ+ identity

3 21st-Century Rights

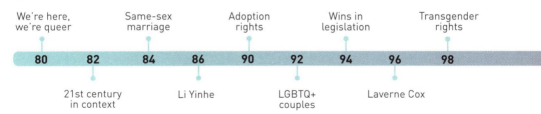

- 80 We're here, we're queer
- 82 21st century in context
- 84 Same-sex marriage
- 86 Li Yinhe
- 90 Adoption rights
- 92 LGBTQ+ couples
- 94 Wins in legislation
- 96 Laverne Cox
- 98 Transgender rights

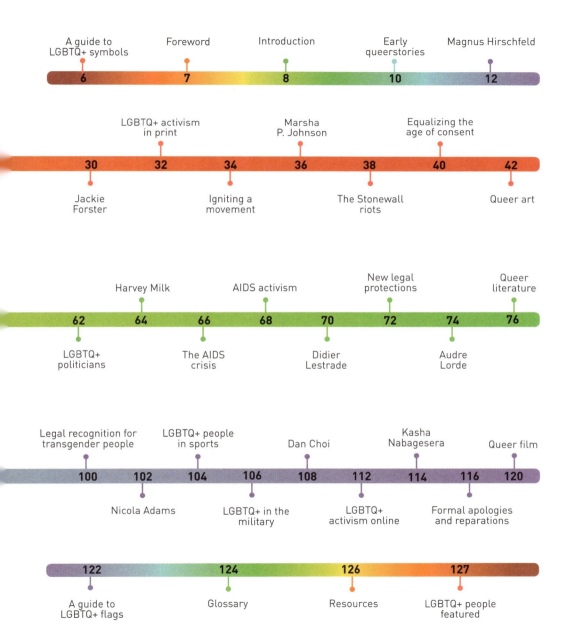

❗ A guide to LGBTQ+ symbols

Throughout history, members of the LGBTQ+ community have used various symbols to express their identity. Some of these symbols, such as rings, handkerchiefs, and flowers, originated as a secret way to indicate sexuality. Today, the LGBTQ+ symbols shown below are worn with pride.

MARS

Two interlocking Mars symbols, each symbolizing the male gender, have been used to represent the gay community since the 1990s.

VENUS

Two interlocking Venus symbols, each of which symbolizes the female gender, have often been used to represent the lesbian community.

TRANSGENDER

Trans activist Holly Boswell combined the Venus and Mars symbols in 1993. Her image is now used to represent the transgender community.

LAMBDA

The Greek letter L, or lambda, was originally associated with the Gay Liberation movement. In 1970, the Gay Activists Alliance in New York adopted it as its official symbol.

PANSEXUAL

The P-shaped symbol of pansexuality unites the male, female and transgender symbols into a new symbol.

PINK TRIANGLE

Originally used in Nazi concentration camps to single out gay men, the pink triangle was reclaimed as a symbol of pride by gay liberation activists in the 1970s.

DOUBLE MOON

Created by Vivian Wagner in 1998, the double moon is an alternative symbol to the pink triangle to represent bisexuality with less problematic associations.

LABRYS

A classical symbol originally representing female strength and independence, the labrys has been used to represent lesbian feminism since the 1970s.

Foreword by Linda Riley

QUEERSTORY: out and proud

At a time when LGBTQ+ rights have progressed beyond expectations, remembering the struggles faced to reach this point in our history feels vital. Understanding the expansive history behind our strong, wonderful, and ever-evolving LGBTQ+ community takes precedence as the fight for LGBTQ+ rights is still ongoing in many parts of the world.

To encompass our entire queer story is an impossible task, but *Queerstory* showcases the integral elements: the activists, artists, and scientists that made an extraordinary difference, paving the path that has moved us forward from the 1940s up until today.

We have reached a place where the future looks brighter than ever and the prospect of overcoming discrimination against LGBTQ+ people feels possible. However, that does not mean that the fight is over by any means—*Queerstory* should inspire us to keep campaigning and breaking down barriers.

Print has played a huge part in LGBTQ+ activism, and as publisher of *DIVA* magazine, my work has played an integral role in bringing queer life into mainstream media, particularly members of the lesbian and bisexual community. This is a topic that I will always feel passionate about as an LGBTQ+ activist, and I am proud that throughout my career I have seen unbelievable achievements.

Our liberation must be celebrated, but the limitations that still remain must not be forgotten. I am filled with hope when I remember that LGBTQ+ marriages are now recognized and laws protect our community. I find comfort knowing there are strong communities and safe spaces for LGBTQ+ people all over the world.

Public acceptance of LGBTQ+ lives remains revolutionary, but we are powerful and determined to gain equality worldwide.

INTRODUCTION

It is difficult to pinpoint the moment at which the LGBTQ+ rights movement began. Long before we might imagine, there were remarkable pioneers like physician Magnus Hirschfeld, who spoke out against popular opinion to question society's mistreatment of queer people and educate the public on what it meant to be nonheterosexual, noncisgender, or nonconforming—often at a time when it was extremely dangerous to do so. However, until the mid-20th century, these were often solitary voices, making radical attempts to communicate their ideas within a climate of deep-rooted discrimination.

By the 1920s in Berlin, there were clubs and newspapers for gay and lesbian people, and some LGBTQ+ individuals had begun to speak out against their oppression, organizing demonstrations and rallies. In the 1930s in New York, the "pansy craze" saw wild underground drag parties sweep the city, inviting a glorious gay subculture onto the main stages of Manhattan. A seed of pride and power was being sown in these discrete celebrations of LGBTQ+ identity across the globe, providing the catalyst for a call to arms across the queer community: to finally come together and demand respect, recognition, and rights.

It was not until the 1940s, however, that LGBTQ+ activists began to effectively mobilize, gaining the strength to begin their formal fight for acceptance. This is where this book really begins, in the aftermath of World War II, at a time when societal norms were beginning to be questioned and the first LGBTQ+ rights organizations were springing up around the world. In the pages that follow, we are taken from the assembly of these "homophile groups" all the way up to the present-day fight for trans rights and formal apologies to the LGBTQ+ community, via the Stonewall riots, the birth of Pride, and activism after the AIDS crisis.

Key Each continent is represented by a different colour throughout the book

- Europe
- Asia
- North America
- South America
- Africa
- Oceania

In any brief history there is a necessary exclusion of many aspects of the story, and this is perhaps particularly true of an account of the fight for LGBTQ+ rights. Even the ever-expanding acronym of "LGBTQ+" struggles to include all the varied groups and individuals it intends to, and the people under its umbrella make up a wide range of separate communities that are sometimes in profound disagreement with each other. This book offers only a selected overview of an overwhelmingly dense and complex movement, powered by countless inspiring individuals and groups who dedicated their lives to a better future for nonheterosexual and noncisgender people.

Above all, the stories, timelines, and biographies collected here serve as an illustration of the incredible resilience, bravery, and optimism of the queer community in the face of discrimination, oppression, and even catastrophe. Together, they are a testament to the great progress made so far and provide a jolt of empowerment to all of us facing the work still to be done.

EARLY QUEERSTORIES

Gender and sexuality have found expression in a variety of diverse ways throughout human history, with evidence existing in almost all ancient civilisations. Some historians suggest that it was not until the arrival of Christian and Islamic influences in the first millennium that queer people faced the kind of prejudices that LGBTQ+ communities are still trying to counter today.

c. 1000 BCE — As long ago as 1000 BCE, it is accepted in early Native American and First Nations cultures that the practice of multiple sex and gender roles and sexuality do not strictly define a person's gender. In 1990, the term **"two-spirit"** is created to encompass all the gender non-conforming terms used by traditional communities.

c. 600 BCE — Ancient Greek lyric poet **SAPPHO**, from the island of Lesbos, writes poems of love and sexual desire. She is praised by Plato and honored in public statues. While many translators and scholars try to heterosexualise her poetry over the years, it is now accepted that her work celebrates love between women.

c. 400 BCE — An Indian text on the art of living, love, and pleasure, the **KAMA SUTRA** is attributed to the ancient Indian philosopher Vātsyāyana. It includes various passages on homosexual relations (both between men and between women) and holds love and sexual fulfilment as one of the primary goals in life.

c. 385 BCE — **PLATO**'s *Symposium* celebrates the practice of homosexual relationships, a standard social norm in ancient Greece. The *Symposium* especially praises the pedagogic benefits of these relationships for adolescents. It is also one of the first works to depict homosexuality as natural rather than as a choice.

c. 10 CE — The **WARREN CUP**, an ornate ancient Roman silver drinking vessel, is decorated with two scenes of male couples engaging in sexual acts against a backdrop of rich tapestries and musical instruments. The cup is most likely commissioned by rich members of a Greek community.

c. 220 CE — The Roman Emperor **ELAGABALUS** is considered by modern historians to have been transgender, as he is reported to have favoured women's clothing and to have offered a vast sum of money to the physician who could perform a sex change operation on him.

c. 450 CE — Surviving texts from Liu Song-dynasty China depict male homosexuality as a normal facet of life in the late third century, explaining that it is such a regular practice that it affects heterosexual marriages and makes women resentful and jealous.

c. 500 CE — The **MAHABHARATA**, a Sanskrit epic poem from ancient India, contains several LGBTQ+ characters. The most well-known of these is the warrior in the Kurukshetra war named Shikhandi—born Shikhandini—who is assigned female at birth but identifies as male, eventually exchanging gender with a forest spirit and marrying a woman.

c. 750 — During the Abbasid Caliphate of the Islamic Empire, Muslim poets such as the Persian-Arab **ABU NUWAS** write lyrical poetry celebrating homosexual love and the charm and beauty of young male lovers.

"Soon the day will come when science will win victory over error, justice a victory over injustice, and human love a victory over human hatred and ignorance."

German-Jewish physician and radical theorist of sexuality and gender Magnus Hirschfeld was one of the most groundbreaking pioneers in the fight for LGBTQ+ rights. Throughout his career, Hirschfeld tirelessly advocated for an acceptance of homosexuality and was the first doctor to research and openly support transgender people, famously supervising Lili Elbe's first sex reassignment surgery in Berlin in 1930. He was revolutionary in his inclusivity, recognising all people across today's understanding of the LGBTQ+ spectrum. In 1897, he established the Scientific-Humanitarian Committee, the world's first gay rights organization, and in 1919, he opened the Institute for Sexual Science, the world's first sexology institute. After the Nazis' rise to power in 1933, Hirschfeld's institute was burned down and his studies confiscated. It has taken over a century for the world to catch up with his progressive work.

Magnus Hirschfeld
German
1868–1935

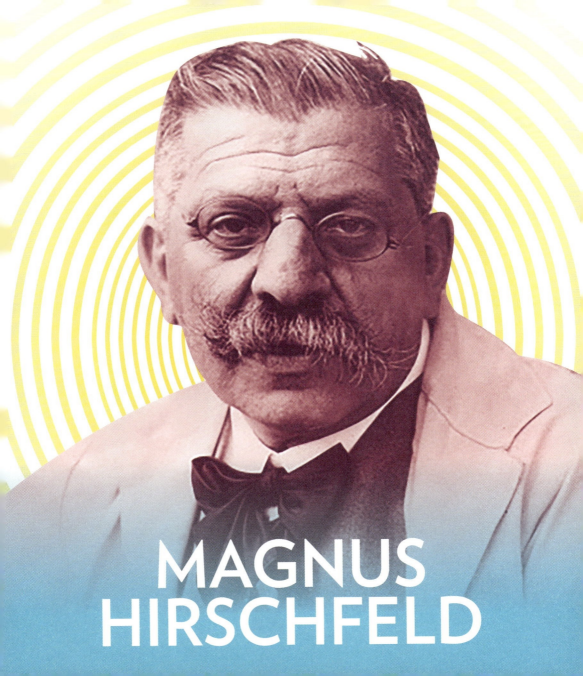

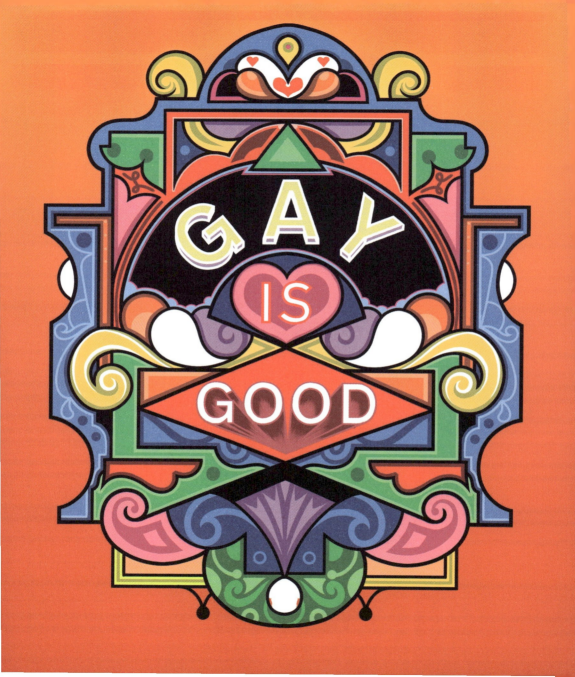

1 Before Stonewall
1940s to 1960s

LGBTQ+ individuals come together to demand:
- the decriminalization of homosexuality
- LGBTQ+ rights
- justice after the Stonewall riots

1947
Lesbian publication and "America's gayest magazine" *Vice Versa* first published

1955
Openly gay singer Billy Wright releases "Don't You Want a Man Like Me?" performed in drag

1952
Christine Jorgensen's sexual reassignment surgery makes the front page of *New York Daily News*

1952
Patricia Highsmith publishes her tale of lesbian love *The Price of Salt* (republished as *Carol*)

GAY IS GOOD

The 1940s to the 1960s were game-changing decades for the international LGBTQ+ rights movement. Despite the criminalization of homosexuality in most countries around the world, gay men and women began to organize themselves formally in the wake of World War II, collaborating across national boundaries to protest their rights to social and legal equality.

These first groups defined themselves as "homophile" organizations, meaning (from the Greek) "loving the same." From the Danish Forbundet af 1948 to the French Arcadie and the US Mattachine Society, these organizations provided a forum for the gay community. In 1968, Frank Kameny's slogan "Gay is Good" was adopted by the North American Conference of Homophile Organizations (NACHO, pronounced "Nay-Ko") delegates, rejecting the idea that being gay was anything to be ashamed of.

Gradually, this work fighting for equality started to bear fruit: Sweden and Denmark both decriminalized homosexuality in 1944; in 1962 the first US state (Illinois) decriminalized consensual sexual relations between same-sex couples; in 1967, England and Wales followed suit with the Sexual Offences Act; East Germany followed in 1968 and West Germany in 1969.

1956
James Baldwin publishes queer novel *Giovanni's Room*

1959
Some Like It Hot is released, featuring cross-dressing and a same-sex kiss

1967
Craig Rodwell opens the world's first gay book store, the Oscar Wilde Memorial Bookshop, in New York

1969
Gay avante-garde theatre group The Cockettes is founded in San Francisco

Alongside these legal wins, a new generation of activists, emboldened by the strategies and progress of the civil rights movement, were changing the direction and tactics of the fight for LGBTQ+ rights. Viewing their struggle as part of a larger picture of dismantling broad social structures of oppression, these activists were more defiant in their outlook and demands. At the same time, the LGBTQ+ community in the US began to resist police raids on gay bars, notably Compton's Cafeteria in San Francisco and LA's Black Cat Tavern.

In 1969, the unrest reached breaking point at the Stonewall Inn in New York's Greenwich Village neighborhood. In an era-defining moment, patrons of the bar and local residents fought back against persecution: A 200-person riot ensued for three nights. The uprising sent a loud message to the world, galvanizing an international movement. In its aftermath, a powerful new force emerged: gay liberation.

1940s TO 1960s IN CONTEXT

From throwing off the yoke of empire to the push for gender and racial equality and the fight against dictators, wars, and the state, the struggle for queer rights was born among the worldwide liberation movements post–World War II.

1939–1945 | WORLD WAR II
World War II (1939–1945) involved and affected almost every country in the world and remains the deadliest conflict in human history with an estimated 70–85 million deaths. This includes an estimated 6 million Jews as well as a still unclear number of homosexuals, thought to be in the thousands, who died during the Holocaust. The USA's development and use of atomic weapons against Japan in 1945 effectively ended the war and led to a nuclear arms race with the Soviet Union in the following decades. With Western Europe recovering from the war, a cold war between the US and the Soviet Union emerged as the two nations competed to be the world's leading superpower.

1945–1960 | POSTWAR DECOLONIZATION
A period of decolonization followed World War II, as nations fought for independence from imperial rule. In India, Gandhi became a global icon for his policy of nonviolent protest, which saw India gain its independence from Britain in 1947. In 1960, since dubbed the "Year of Africa," seventeen countries gained independence from their European colonial rulers. The transition to self-governance was often violent, and the legacy of colonial rule is visible in discriminatory antigay legislation that, in some cases, exists to this day.

1964 | THE CIVIL RIGHTS ACT
The decades-long struggle for equal rights for African Americans won its largest legislative gains during the 1960s. The movement used nonviolent strategies such as boycotts, sit-ins, and marches to achieve its goals. The Civil Rights Act of 1964 banned discrimination based on race, color, religion, sex, or national origin and ended segregation. That same year, Rev. Martin Luther King, Jr. won the Nobel Peace Prize for his leadership of the movement.

1968
SOCIAL AND POLITICAL UNREST
The year 1968 was marked by popular rebellion and social unrest, with violent protests against authorities and elites taking place in most European capitals, including Paris, London, Rome, Prague, and Berlin, as well as in the US. While there is still much debate on the legacy of the 1968 riots, they are widely regarded as the archetype for the modern protest.

1969
FIRST MAN ON THE MOON
American astronaut Neil Armstrong was the first person to walk on the moon during the Apollo 11 mission in 1969. As part of the Cold War Space Race between the Soviet Union and the USA, the mission was preceded by other great achievements: The first person in space was Russian Yuri Gagarin in 1961, soon followed by the first woman in 1963, Valentina Tereshkova.

1969
THE COUNTERCULTURE MOVEMENT
The Woodstock festival is considered the peak of the antiestablishment counterculture movement that took place in much of the Western world during the 1960s and 1970s. Made up of young people, often born during the postwar baby boom, the counterculture was opposed to the mainstream views of contemporary society, promoting free love, women's rights, and a restructuring of traditional economic and family systems.

1960–1979
SECOND-WAVE FEMINISM
Second-wave feminism fought for women's rights within the family, reproductive rights, and against legal inequalities. By giving women control over their reproductive health, the increased availability of the contraceptive pill throughout the 1960s was instrumental in giving women the choice to have children, further education, and a career. A major victory for the women's movement came in 1973 when the US Supreme Court protected a woman's right to have an abortion in the now famous *Roe vs. Wade* trial. However, second-wave feminism has been criticized for failing to include the experiences of lesbian and trans women.

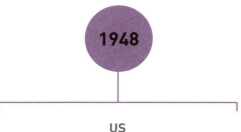

US

BIOLOGIST AND SEXOLOGIST ALFRED KINSEY PUBLISHES THE KINSEY SCALE, REVOLUTIONIZING POPULAR THINKING ON SEXUALITY: SEXUAL ATTRACTION HAD PREVIOUSLY BEEN THOUGHT TO BE FIXED AND BINARY. KINSEY PRESENTS ATTRACTION AS FLUID, AND SUBJECT TO CHANGE.

THE WORLD IS NOT TO BE DIVIDED INTO SHEEP AND GOATS. NOT ALL THINGS ARE BLACK NOR ALL THINGS WHITE.

ALFRED KINSEY (1894–1956)
AMERICAN BIOLOGIST, SEXOLOGIST AND
'FATHER OF THE SEXUAL REVOLUTION'

1948

DENMARK

AXEL AXGIL FOUNDS KRESDEN AF 1948 ('CIRCLE OF 1948'), ONE OF THE FIRST LGBTQ+ RIGHTS ORGANIZATIONS IN THE WORLD. IT IS NOW KNOWN AS LGBT DENMARK.

1950

FRANCE

ANDRÉ BAUDRY SETS UP THE FIRST HOMOPHILE GROUP IN FRENCH HISTORY, THE ASSOCIATION ARCADIE. IT WORKS TO SOCIALIZE THE ACCEPTANCE OF THE GAY COMMUNITY IN FRENCH SOCIETY WITH ITS OWN CLUB HOUSE AND LITERARY REVIEW.

1950

US

THE MATTACHINE SOCIETY FORMED BY HARRY HAY IS ONE OF THE FIRST GAY RIGHTS GROUPS IN THE UNITED STATES, FOLLOWED FIVE YEARS LATER BY THE FIRST NATIONAL LESBIAN RIGHTS ORGANIZATION, THE DAUGHTERS OF BILITIS (DOB).

1951

THE INTERNATIONAL COMMITTEE FOR SEXUAL EQUALITY (ICSE) IS FOUNDED BY THE PRESIDENT OF DUTCH HOMOPHILE ORGANIZATION, THE CENTER FOR CULTURE AND LEISURE (COC), UNITING EUROPEAN AND US HOMOPHILE ORGANIZATIONS IN A TRANSNATIONAL RIGHTS GROUP.

"Be open. Come out. Keep fighting. This is the only way to move anything."

Born in 1915, Axel Axgil was a true pioneer of the LGBTQ+ movement. A founding member of Kresden af 1948, under his stewardship, the organization amassed 1,339 members by 1951 and reached a world record of 2,600 by the time he stepped down as chairman in 1952. He campaigned for the right to enter into a civil partnership for decades and was also one half of the first same-sex couple in the world to enter into a registered partnership, having been engaged to his partner for almost forty years. When they finally married in 1989, Axel and his partner, Eigil Eskildsen, merged their first names to create the new surname "Axgil".

Axel Axgil
DANISH

1915–2011

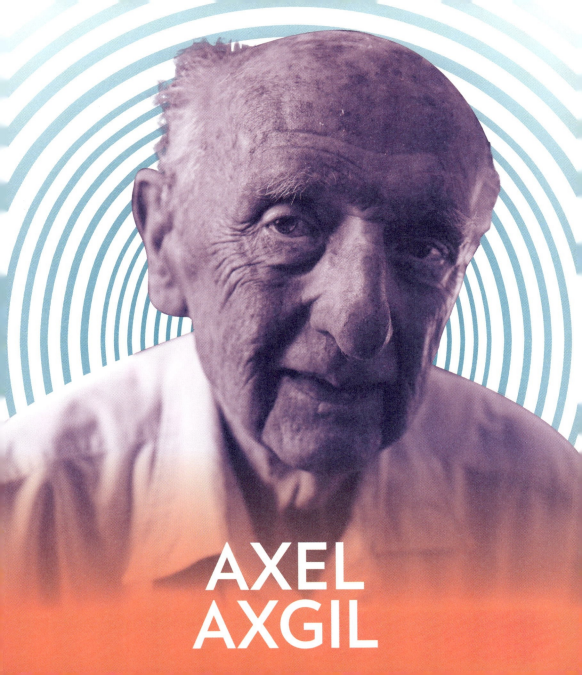

1957

UK

THE WOLFENDEN REPORT IS PUBLISHED, RECOMMENDING THAT "HOMOSEXUAL BEHAVIOR BETWEEN CONSENTING ADULTS IN PRIVATE SHOULD NO LONGER BE A CRIMINAL OFFENCE." IT LEADS TO THE PASSING OF THE SEXUAL OFFENCES ACT, WHICH LEGALLY DECRIMINALIZES HOMOSEXUALITY IN 1967.

1958

EAST GERMANY

PROMINENT PSYCHOLOGIST RUDOLF KLIMMER USES HIS INFLUENCE TO STOP ALL CONVICTIONS FOR SEXUAL ORIENTATION AND SUCCESSFULLY PUSHES FOR LEGALIZATION IN 1968.

EQUALITY MEANS MORE THAN PASSING LAWS. THE STRUGGLE IS REALLY WON IN THE HEARTS AND MINDS OF THE COMMUNITY, WHERE IT REALLY COUNTS.

BARBARA GITTINGS 1932-2007
AMERICAN ACTIVIST
FOR LGBTQ+ EQUALITY

DECRIMINALIZING HOMOSEXUALITY

Anti-gay stigma has been entrenched in law in many countries around the world. Thanks to the efforts of many brave and tireless campaigners, these laws have gradually been overturned. The chart below shows a selection of the dates of decriminalization.

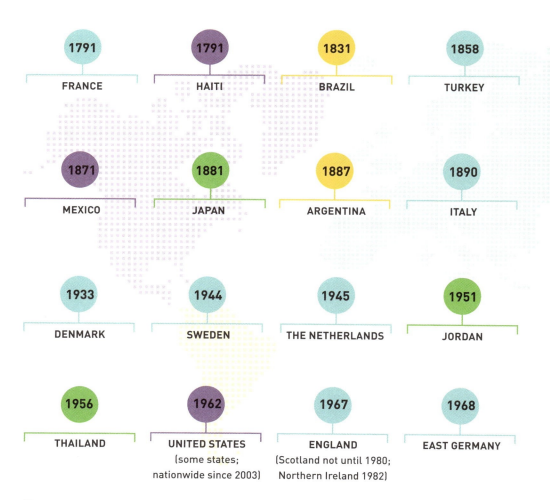

| 1791 | 1791 | 1831 | 1858 |
| FRANCE | HAITI | BRAZIL | TURKEY |

| 1871 | 1881 | 1887 | 1890 |
| MEXICO | JAPAN | ARGENTINA | ITALY |

| 1933 | 1944 | 1945 | 1951 |
| DENMARK | SWEDEN | THE NETHERLANDS | JORDAN |

| 1956 | 1962 | 1967 | 1968 |
| THAILAND | UNITED STATES (some states; nationwide since 2003) | ENGLAND (Scotland not until 1980; Northern Ireland 1982) | EAST GERMANY |

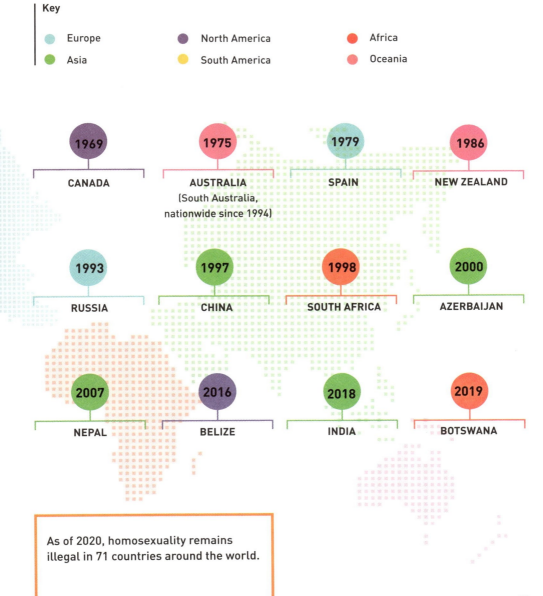

> "Women are blessed with two entirely separate systems; one is there for their sexuality . . . the other for reproduction. There's no need to get them mixed up."

Born in London in 1926, Jackie Forster was a broadcaster, reporter, and trailblazing lesbian rights activist. After publicly coming out at Speaker's Corner in London in 1969, Forster joined the Campaign for Homosexual Equality (CHE) and dedicated the rest of her life to fighting for LGBTQ+ rights. In 1972 she cofounded the lesbian social group Sappho, which published a monthly magazine until 1981 and held weekly meetings until the late 1980s. She campaigned for the rights of lesbians to become mothers through artificial insemination, and cowrote *Rocking the Cradle* about lesbian mothers with Gill Hanscombe in 1981. Hanscombe described Forster as being "that rare individual. She has noble instincts and the noblest of them is to fight for injustice of any kind, not just for lesbians."

Jackie Forster
ENGLISH

1926–1998

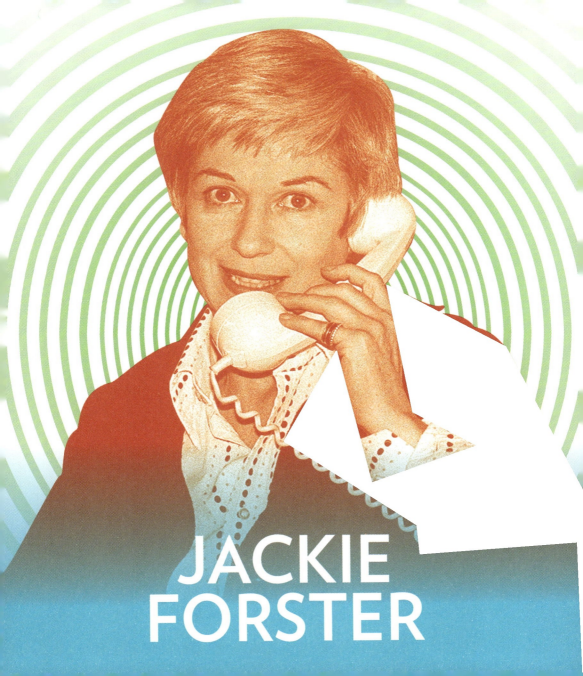

LGBTQ+ ACTIVISM IN PRINT

Magazines played an important role in rallying the LGBTQ+ rights movement and creating solidarity in communities that faced prejudice from the mainstream media.

1896 — German writer and anarchist **ADOLF BRAND** publishes the first gay magazine in the world, *Der Eigene* (*The Unique*), an arts and culture magazine that runs for thirty-five years, finally ceasing publication because of the Nazis in the 1930s. Brand is also a member of the first ever LGBTQ+ rights organization, Magnus Hirschfeld's Scientific-Humanitarian Committee.

1924 — Germany is also responsible for the first lesbian magazine in the world, *Die Freundin* (*The Girlfriend*), which is published in Berlin until 1933, when it is forced to shut down by the Nazis. Part-educational, part-political, the magazine mainly publishes short stories and novellas. It aims at creating a community of lesbians, publishing articles about nightspots and cultural events as well as personal ads.

1952 — In the postwar years in Japan, a number of gay groups begin to network. A prominent group is the Adonis club, which for ten years publishes a newsletter featuring cultural essays, erotic material, and personal ads. **YUKIO MISHIMA** is one its contributors. It is an essential precursor of 1970s LGBTQ+ magazines in Japan, such as *Barazoku* and *Adon*.

1953 — The first gay men's magazine in the US, *One*, is published. Founded in 1952, **ONE, INC.** was born from a discussion of the Mattachine Society. The magazine is sold publicly in Los Angeles and One, Inc. wins a lawsuit against the US Post Office department when it refuses to distribute the magazine on the grounds of obscenity. The One Archives is now one of the oldest LGBTQ+ archive institutions.

1956 San Francisco–based lesbian organization the **DAUGHTERS OF BILITIS** publishes the first issue of *The Ladder* magazine, which continues until 1972. While it starts as a twelve-page newsletter, its circulation grows quickly. With Barbara Gittings as editor in 1963, it becomes overtly political.

1964 The first gay rights organization **ASK** emerges in Canada and the Toronto magazine *Gay* is launched. This is the first magazine to use the word "gay" in its title. It is soon expanded to the US as *Gay International*. But it only lasts two years, shutting down in 1966 due to criminal charges against one of its creators.

1967 The monthly single-page newsletter published by radical gay rights organization **PRIDE** (Personal Rights in Defense and Education) evolves into a newspaper known as *The Advocate*. It is the longest running LGBTQ+ magazine in the US.

1972 *Gay News*, Britain's first gay newspaper, is founded in London and later relaunched in magazine format as the *Gay Times*. It is now published both in the UK and the US. The same year sees the launch of the influential British lesbian magazine *Sappho*, founded by 12 women including Jackie Forster, which is circulated until 1981.

1975 The most enduring gay publication in Australia, *Campaign*, is launched just as South Australia finally decriminalizes homosexuality. Its name plays on the "camp" in "campaign" and its content spans news, political manifestos, event listings, polemic, advertisements, celebrity interviews, and photos and gossip.

1979 French magazine *Gai Pied* is founded. The publication is supported by a number of prominent intellectuals who protect the magazine against censorship and often contribute, including Michel Foucault, Serge Gainsbourg, David Hockney, and Jean-Paul Sartre. Nevertheless, the minister of the interior threatens to shut the magazine down in 1987; this move is met with protest from many quarters and the minister of culture declares his public support. Circulation ends in 1992.

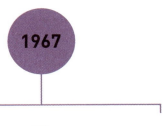

1967

US

PLAIN-CLOTHES POLICE OFFICERS RAID THE BLACK CAT TAVERN IN LOS ANGELES ON NEW YEAR'S DAY. THE RAID PROMPTS A SERIES OF PROTESTS ORGANIZED BY PRIDE (PERSONAL RIGHTS IN DEFENSE AND EDUCATION), MARKING THE FIRST TIME "PRIDE" IS ASSOCIATED WITH THE LGBTQ+ RIGHTS MOVEMENT.

1969

AUSTRALIA

THE ACT HOMOSEXUAL LAW REFORM SOCIETY IS FORMED, A HUMANIST ORGANIZATION BASED IN CANBERRA THAT IS CONSIDERED AUSTRALIA'S FIRST GAY RIGHTS ORGANIZATION.

1969

US

POLICE RAID THE STONEWALL INN, GREENWICH VILLAGE, AS PART OF A SERIES OF VIOLENT CRACKDOWNS ON GAY BARS SERVING WITHOUT A LICENSE TO SERVE ALCOHOL. THE QUEER COMMUNITY FIGHTS BACK, AND THE UPRISING LASTS SIX DAYS, TRIGGERING THE MODERN LGBTQ+ LIBERATION MOVEMENT IN THE US AND BEYOND.

1971

FRANCE

INSPIRED BY PROTEST MOVEMENTS WORLDWIDE, THE HOMOSEXUAL FRONT FOR REVOLUTIONARY ACTION IS FOUNDED, ONE OF THE FIRST RADICAL GAY LIBERATION GROUPS IN FRANCE.

IGNITING A MOVEMENT

"Darling, I want my gay rights now!"

An outspoken visionary and trailblazing trans, gay liberation, and AIDS activist, "true Drag Mother" and key participant in the Stonewall uprising of 1969 Marsha P. Johnson was one of the architects of the modern LGBTQ+ rights movement. Some credit her with having thrown the first brick in the Stonewall rebellion of 1969, the pivotal protest in which the queer community fought back following a summer of violent and humiliating police raids. In its aftermath, Johnson helped to organize the gay liberation marches in New York that would become Pride; together with Sylvia Rivera, she also established Street Transvestite Action Revolutionaries (STAR) in 1970, an inspirational collective that provided housing and support to homeless queer teens and sex workers in lower Manhattan. When asked, she said the P in her name meant "Pay It No Mind," a defiant epithet that rejected gender binaries. She continued to organize and fight for LGBTQ+ rights, joining the AIDS advocacy group ACT UP in 1987, until her death in 1992, when her body was found in the Hudson River.

Marsha P. Johnson
AMERICAN

1945–1992

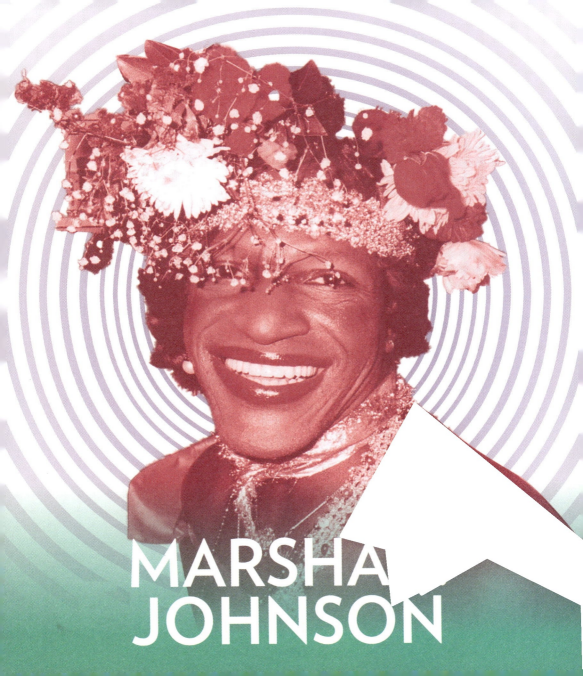

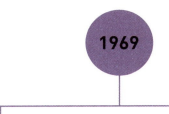

US

IN THE WAKE OF THE STONEWALL RIOTS, THE GAY LIBERATION FRONT (GLF) IS FORMED IN NEW YORK IN 1969. ITS AIM IS TO DISMANTLE SOCIAL INSTITUTIONS SUCH AS GENDER AND THE NUCLEAR FAMILY AND ACHIEVE SEXUAL LIBERATION FOR ALL. IT IS THE FIRST ORGANIZATION TO USE THE WORD "GAY" IN ITS NAME.

WE CAN NO LONGER STAY INVISIBLE. WE SHOULD NOT BE ASHAMED OF WHO WE ARE. WE HAVE TO SHOW THE WORLD THAT WE ARE NUMEROUS.

SYLVIA RIVERA (1951–2002)
AMERICAN GAY LIBERATION AND TRANS RIGHTS ACTIVIST WHO PLAYED A KEY ROLE IN THE STONEWALL UPRISING

EQUALIZING THE AGE OF CONSENT

To date, 180 countries have brought the age of consent for LGBTQ+ individuals into harmony with the age of consent for heterosexual sex. In some countries, the law is ambiguous, making no distinction between hetero- and homosexual acts.

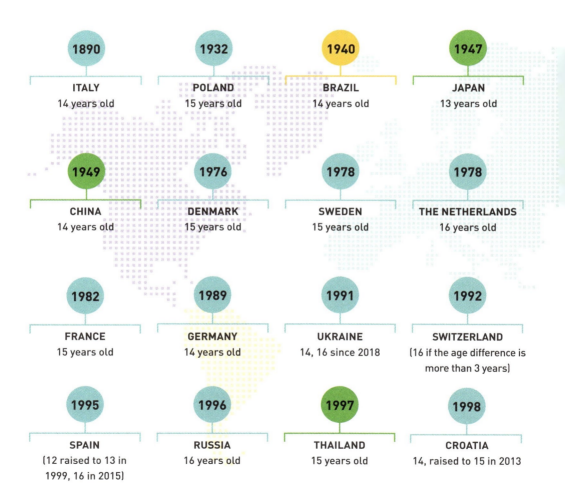

1890 ITALY — 14 years old

1932 POLAND — 15 years old

1940 BRAZIL — 14 years old

1947 JAPAN — 13 years old

1949 CHINA — 14 years old

1976 DENMARK — 15 years old

1978 SWEDEN — 15 years old

1978 THE NETHERLANDS — 16 years old

1982 FRANCE — 15 years old

1989 GERMANY — 14 years old

1991 UKRAINE — 14, 16 since 2018

1992 SWITZERLAND — (16 if the age difference is more than 3 years)

1995 SPAIN — (12 raised to 13 in 1999, 16 in 2015)

1996 RUSSIA — 16 years old

1997 THAILAND — 15 years old

1998 CROATIA — 14, raised to 15 in 2013

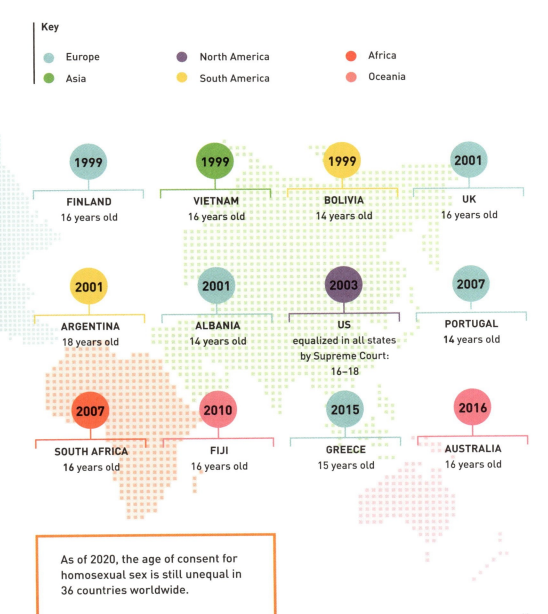

QUEER ART

Many LGBTQ+ artists have used their work to explore the relationships between gender, sexuality, and identity. Challenging society's traditionally held views, they have portrayed the world around them and, in doing so, have actively shaped it.

1930 Part of the Dada movement in Germany during the time of the Weimar Republic, **HANNAH HÖCH** pioneers the photomontage technique, using images from newspapers and magazines to criticize her society's gender roles and encourage women's liberation. Her 1930 work *Marlene* is one of her most controversial photomontages, representing a sexually ambiguous subject. Höch's work is censored by the Nazi regime, which considers it "degenerate" art.

1945 Established as a foremost postwar painter after his 1945 exhibition of *Three Studies for Figures at the Base of a Crucifixion*, **FRANCIS BACON** is a British artist living openly as a homosexual before it is legalized in the UK in 1967. Throughout his life, he has a series of public affairs that inspire and feature in a number of his works.

1967 **DAVID HOCKNEY** becomes one of the most popular and influential British artists of the twentieth century. He rises to fame during the 1960s, painting honest depictions of gay love such as *Man in Shower*, *Domestic Scene*, and *Peter Getting out of Nick's Pool*, which wins the 1967 John Moores Painting Prize.

1982 **KEITH HARING**'s 1982 *Untitled*, depicting two figures with a heart motif, has been interpreted as a representation of homosexual love and is a perfect example of Haring's vibrant, energetic, graffiti-inspired artworks, dealing with the most complex political issues, and which become symbols of a generation. In 1988, Haring is diagnosed with AIDS and spends the remaining years of his life dedicated to increasing activism and awareness about the disease.

1988 — Born in the suburbs of Melbourne, Australia, **LEIGH BOWERY** spends most of his adult life in London, where his flamboyant personal style and taboo-breaking performance art make him an iconic figure of the late 1980s avant-garde scene, first performing in 1988. From 1990 until his death from an AIDS-related illness in 1994, Bowery is a model and muse for Lucian Freud, Freud having seen his performance at the Anthony d'Offay Gallery. Bowery's fearless creativity inspires a generation of artists and performers, from Boy George and Alexander McQueen to Vivienne Westwood and Lady Gaga.

2002 — **ZANELE MUHOLI** is a South African artist and visual activist. They rise to prominence in the 2000s for their intimate and powerful portraits depicting black LGBTQ+ individuals, holding their first solo exhibition in Johannesburg in 2002. Muholi sees themselves as a visual activist and art as a tool for social empowerment and visibility. In 2002, Muholi cofounds the Forum for the Empowerment of Women, a black lesbian organization dedicated to providing a safe space for women to meet and organize events. In 2009 they found Inkanyiso, a nonprofit organization concerned with queer visual activism.

2014 — Chinese photographer and poet **REN HANG**'s work reaches a global audience following his first solo exhibition in Copenhagen in 2014. His work is significant for its representation of sexuality in a heavily censored society. He is arrested several times for the erotic undertones in his nude photographs, which show frank depictions of LGBTQ+ love. Hang takes his own life at the age of 29, but his art opens a window on sexual freedom in a conservative society.

2018 — **KEHINDE WILEY** uses the visual vocabulary of old European portraits, replacing the subjects with black men. By using a medium that historically invoked glory and prestige, Wiley seeks to challenge existing stereotypes in American society. In 2018, Wiley becomes the first black—and first openly gay—artist to paint an official presidential portrait when Barack Obama chooses him.

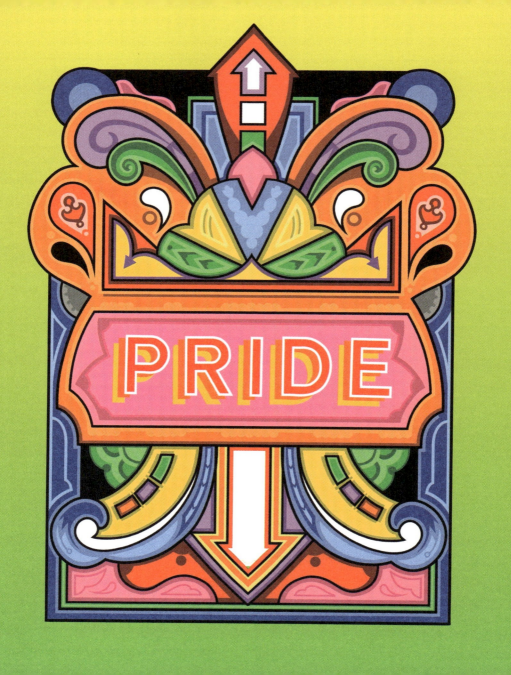

2 LGBTQ+ Liberation
1970s to 1990s

LGBTQ+ communities gain strength and recognition across the globe:
- first pride marches
- LGBTQ+ legislation
- AIDS activism
- achieving political office

1972

That Certain Summer depicts the first gay lovers on TV

1977
On the primetime TV series *Soap*, Billy Crystal plays a gay man

1978
Village People release "Y.M.C.A.," an instant gay anthem

1982
One of the main characters on *Dynasty* comes out as gay to his family

PRIDE

The last 30 years of the 20th century brought highs and lows for the LGBTQ+ community. Considerable progress was made in terms of rights and freedoms but the arrival of AIDS threatened to reverse many of the gains made in social acceptance.

The Gay Liberation Front (GLF) in both the UK and USA worked collaboratively with feminist and civil rights groups through this period. In New York, Stonewall veterans Sylvia Rivera and Marsha P. Johnson founded Street Transvestite Action Revolutionaries (STAR) in 1970, the first trans youth shelter in North America. In 1972, Sweden became the first country to allow trans people to legally change their sex; Chile followed in 1974. These wins fed a narrative of liberation and hope. By 1980, twenty-two US states had ended all restrictions on sexual relations between consenting adults.

The 1980s brought the devastation of the AIDS pandemic, which affected LGBTQ+ people in huge numbers and threw continuing homophobia into sharp relief. In Europe, the press demonized those who had the "gay plague," and in the US the Reagan government ignored the crisis. In the face of such silence, activist groups were formed to put pressure on hastening the development of treatments and services for those diagnosed with HIV/AIDS. The AIDS Coalition to Unleash Power (ACT UP) was established in the US in 1987. Under the banner "Silence=Death," its actions prompted the FDA to

1993
Philadelphia is the first Hollywood film to deal with homophobia and AIDS

1994
An Ikea ad shows an ordinary gay couple for the first time in TV advertising

1997
Ellen DeGeneres comes out on the cover of *Time* magazine

2000
Hilary Swank wins an Oscar for her portrayal of trans man Brandon Teena in *Boys Don't Cry*

speed up approval processes for treatment. In 1987, an estimated 750,000 people took part in the Second National March on Washington for Lesbian and Gay Rights in protest at the government's handling of the AIDS crisis and lack of progress on gay rights. The date of the march, October 11, has been celebrated as National Coming Out Day since 1988.

In the 1990s, LGBTQ+ rights activism continued to affirm that queer rights are human rights, focusing on fighting discrimination and pushing for legal protection and equality. Even as positive changes were enshrined in law, progress was not straightforward, calling for the formation of new action groups to draw attention to continuing homophobia and transphobia, which often took the form of antigay violence. One such group, QueerNation, was founded in New York City in 1990. Famous for its confrontational tactics, this grassroots organization reclaimed the word "queer." That same year, Peter Tatchell formed OutRage! Calling for "protection not persecution," the group protested against the huge rise in gay and bisexual men being arrested for consenting, victimless behavior.

These organizations drew attention to continuing problems and national governments began to introduce protective legislation, such as the right to asylum for LGBTQ+ people, granted by Canada and the US in 1994. In 1999, Brazil became the first country in the world to ban conversion therapy—treatment based on "curing" homosexuality.

1970S TO 1990S IN CONTEXT

As queer culture and lifestyles began to become visible in the mainstream and slowly gain wider acceptance, particularly in the western world, there were still huge strides to be made in the battle to achieve equality.

1973

GLAM ROCK
Originating in the UK in the early 1970s, glam rock is characterized by performers wearing deliberately outrageous costumes, makeup, and hair. The flamboyant styles were often androgynous and subverted typical gender roles. David Bowie and Elton John were two of the most famous proponents of glam rock, but the genre's influence was widespread.

1975

THE FALL OF SAIGON
In April 1975, Saigon, the capital of South Vietnam, was captured by the People's Army of Vietnam and the Viet Cong. Referred to as the Liberation of Saigon by the Socialist Republic of Vietnam, the event marked the end of the twenty-year conflict between North and South Vietnam and signaled the beginning of the reunification of the country.

1979

MARGARET THATCHER
Margaret Thatcher became Britain's first female prime minister in 1979. Throughout the 1980s, she was frequently described as the most powerful woman in the world, her uncompromising politics earning her the nickname the "Iron Lady." She enjoyed a close political relationship with US president Ronald Reagan, based on their shared conservative ideals and belief in free-market economics.

1981

HIV/AIDS
AIDS was first reported in 1981 with five cases in the US. In 1982, as similar cases appeared—all with impaired immune systems—the disease was named AIDS, "Acquired Immune Deficiency Syndrome." Since then, AIDS has killed thirty-five million people worldwide. The LGBTQ+ community was seriously affected by AIDS and misconceptions about the disease's connection to homosexuality resulted in social stigmatization. Today, the HIV virus that causes AIDS is treatable, and people with HIV can live long and healthy lives.

1989 | TIANANMEN SQUARE MASSACRE
On June 4, 1989, the Chinese government declared martial law. Troops armed with rifles and tanks fired at demonstrators in what is now known as the Tiananmen Square Massacre, causing thousands of deaths. Among the reasons cited were the weeks of student-led demonstrations that had been held in the Beijing square, in protest against the one-party system and for democracy, freedom of speech, and freedom of the press.

1989 | THE END OF THE COLD WAR
Following a wave of revolutions overthrowing Soviet rule in Central and Eastern Europe, the Berlin Wall—so long a symbol of political division between East and West—was pulled down. The dissolution of the Soviet Union in 1991 ended the Cold War. New freedoms for LGBTQ+ communities in the former Soviet Union followed. In 1993, under pressure from the Council of Europe, Russia decriminalized homosexuality alongside other former Soviet states: Ukraine in 1991, Estonia and Latvia in 1992, Lithuania in 1993, Belarus in 1994, and Moldova in 1995.

1990s | DIGITAL TECHNOLOGY
The World Wide Web, a key tool of the information age, became available to the general public in 1991. The growth of the internet contributed to a period of unprecedented globalization, allowing faster communication around the world. Through the emergence of social media, LGBTQ+ people have been able to build online communities with people from disparate geographies, diminishing the isolation that had previously been a part of the LGBTQ+ experience.

1994 | END OF APARTHEID
In 1990, the F.W. de Klerk government began the process of ending apartheid, releasing Nelson Mandela after twenty-seven years in prison for opposing racial segregation. The first election with universal adult suffrage followed in 1994, and Nelson Mandela became South Africa's first nonwhite president. In his inaugural speech he declared South Africa would provide equal protection for all its citizens regardless of "color, gender, religion, political opinion, or sexual orientation."

1970

US

ON JUNE 28, PEOPLE RETURN TO THE STONEWALL INN TO MARK THE ANNIVERSARY OF THE RIOTS. THEY CALL IT "CHRISTOPHER STREET LIBERATION DAY," CELEBRATING WITH A MARCH IN NEW YORK AND A PARADE IN LOS ANGELES. THESE CELEBRATIONS SERVE AS A CATALYST TO OTHER GAY PRIDE MARCHES ACROSS THE GLOBE.

> **WE MUST ROOT OUT THE IDEA THAT HOMOSEXUALITY IS BAD, SICK OR IMMORAL, AND DEVELOP A GAY PRIDE.**
>
> **THE 1971 GAY LIBERATION FRONT MANIFESTO**

"We were sexual liberationists and social revolutionaries, out to turn the world upside down."

Australia-born Peter Tatchell first came to prominence as a leading member of the London Gay Liberation Front in the early 1970s, organizing sit-ins and protests against institutionalized homophobia in the UK. He has since taken this fight for equality across the world, taking part in countless direct-action campaigns in the advocation for queer rights. During the AIDS pandemic he published the first self-help guide for people with HIV and fought for the human rights of those who had been infected. In 2010, a blue plaque was mounted on his London home, celebrating forty years of defending human rights. Tatchell currently spends his time actively supporting human rights and liberation movements worldwide, as he has done throughout his entire life.

Peter Tatchell
BRITISH-AUSTRALIAN

1952–

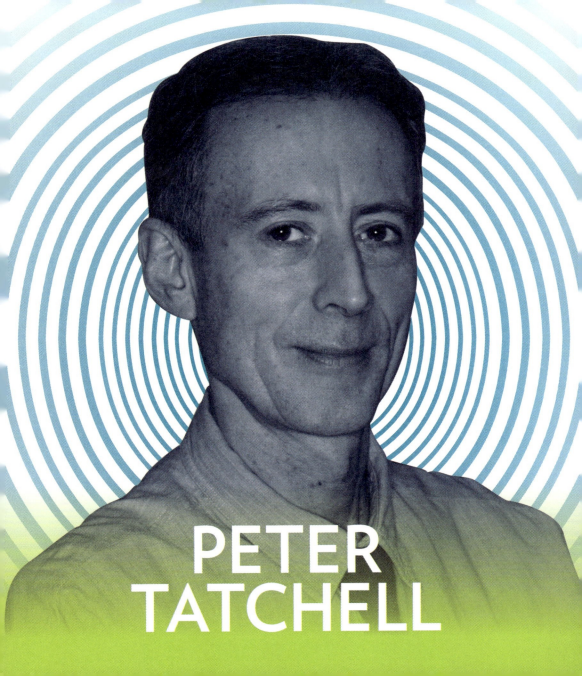

QUEER THEORY

Queer theory is based on the idea that gender is socially constructed and encompasses all sexual acts and identities that are not heteronormative. Feminist and film theorist Teresa de Lauretis coined the term in 1990 at her conference "Queer Theory: Gay and Lesbian Sexualities" at the University of California, using the expression to redefine the terms we use to define sexuality.

1976 — French philosopher and historian of ideas **MICHEL FOUCAULT** publishes the first volume of his *History of Sexuality* in France in 1976. Adopting a constructivist position, he persuasively indicates that the birth of "homosexuality" dates as a category to the 1870s, arguing that there was no prior corresponding category defining people for those acts. While those acts were indeed condemned (both by religious and civil law), they were not labeled or categorized, in other words those acts were not indicative of a specific "identity."

1990 — American philosopher and gender theorist **JUDITH BUTLER** is known for challenging traditional conceptions of gender and developing the pivotal theory of gender performativity. She has published extensively; her main works include *Gender Trouble* (1990), *Bodies That Matter* (1993), and *Undoing Gender* (2004). The underlining idea in Butler's work is that all categories we use are essentially socially constructed: Gender, rather than being the expression of an "essence," is performative.

1990 — American scholar **EVE KOSOFSKY SEDGWICK**'s work as a queer theorist draws mainly from literature as a space in which to identify queer potential. Some of her most notable works include *Between Men: English Literature and Male Homosocial Desire* (1985) and *Epistemology of the Closet* (1990), in which she discusses the homosexual/heterosexual binary to underline the incoherencies of attempting a definition of homosexuality as an issue of importance for a minority rather then a determining issue for all.

1998

American author, professor, and philosopher **JACK HALBERSTAM**, also known as **JUDITH HALBERSTAM**, publishes *Female Masculinity*, in which she theorizes the "bathroom problem," where gender binarism is at its clearest and strictest, offering no place for people who don't fit into those categories. In 2001, she published *The Queer Art of Failure*, in which she argued that failing to live up to heteronormative standards offers room for freedom and creativity.

1999

With the publication of *Disentifications: Queers of Color and the Politics of Performance*, Cuban-American academic **JOSÉ ESTEBAN MUÑOZ** highlights the importance of issues of race and ethnicity within queer studies, a perspective often neglected by the field since its emergence in the 1990s. Muñoz went beyond sexuality and introduced the angles of race and identity, focusing on the ways in which queer artists of color take on, and at the same time, subvert and modify stereotypes. His other seminal work, *Cruising Utopia: The Then and There of Queer Futurity* (2009), sets an optimistic basis for the future of queer communities, which relies on the potential of queer performance art to indicate a utopian futurity.

2000

American professor **ROSEMARY HENNESSY** publishes *Profit and Pleasure*. Taking a materialist approach to sexuality, her queer theory is strictly connected to the structures of late capitalism. She argues that identities that have always been linked to sexuality, such as gender, nationality, and race, are in fact a product of capitalism. Hennessey suggests that, while queers have more and more freedom of expression, capitalist society still relies on a traditional binary division of labor.

2004

American literary critic **LEE EDELMAN**'s *No Future: Queer Theory and the Death Drive* studies the state of a society marked by "reproductive futurism," where the child is the ultimate political referent holding together the present and the future, and where all theory is aimed at a better future. He introduces the figure of the sinthomosexual, disinterested in the future of humanity because of their reproductive incapability, refusing the futurist appeal to the child and embodying the death drive.

PRIDE EVENTS AROUND THE WORLD

The first Pride event was organized by the Gay Liberation Front to commemorate the Stonewall riots. Today, Pride is celebrated in numerous countries around the world, with an annual parade to celebrate LGBTQ+ culture, achievements, and legal rights. The map below shows a selection of them and the year in which each held its first Pride parade.

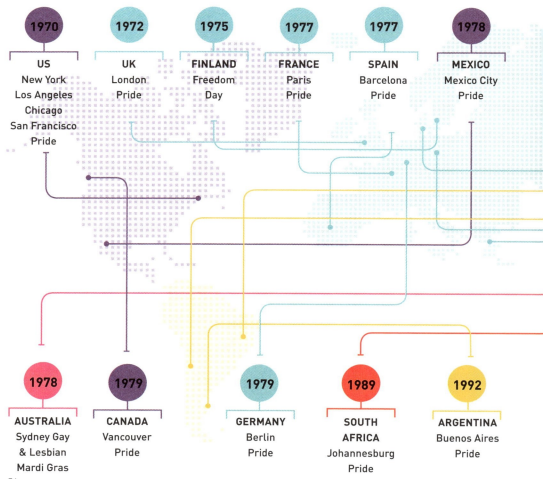

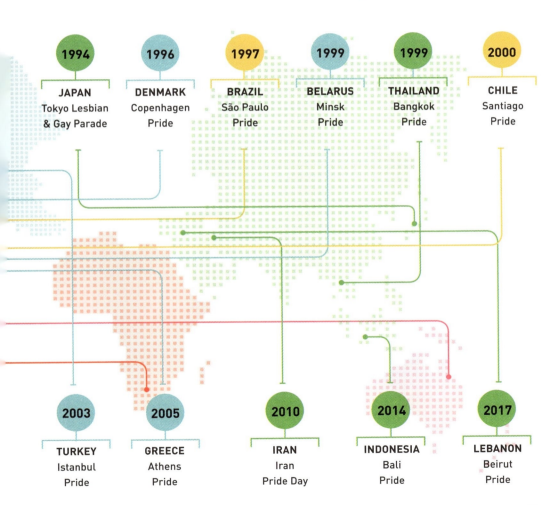

"Bi, Poly, Switch—I'm not greedy, I know what I want."

Born in the Bronx, New York, Brenda Howard advocated for LGBTQ+ rights and the inclusion of bisexuality in the early stages of the movement from the time of the Stonewall Inn events until her death. She was the main organizer of the first Pride week in June 1970 and the Christopher Street Liberation Day parade that became its landmark event. She laid the grounds for other parades around the world and became known as the "Mother of Pride." A militant activist for all minorities, Howard advocated for causes such as health care, women and people of color's rights, and HIV/AIDS. She was arrested multiple times during her protests. In 1988 she founded the New York Area Bisexual Network and successfully advocated for the inclusion of bisexuality in the 1993 march on Washington.

Brenda Howard
AMERICAN

1946–2005

1972

ITALY

THE FIRST PUBLIC DEMONSTRATION IN DEFENSE OF LGBTQ+ RIGHTS IN ITALY IS ORGANIZED BY FUORI, THE FIRST ITALIAN ORGANIZATION FOR GAY RIGHTS (FOUNDED THE PREVIOUS YEAR), TO PROTEST AGAINST A CATHOLIC-INSPIRED CONFERENCE ON SEXUAL DEVIANCE.

1972

SWEDEN

SWEDEN DECLASSIFIES TRANSVESTISM AS AN ILLNESS AND BECOMES THE FIRST COUNTRY IN THE WORLD TO ALLOW TRANSGENDER PEOPLE TO LEGALLY CHANGE THEIR SEX.

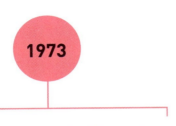

1973

AUSTRALIA AND NEW ZEALAND

THE AUSTRALIAN AND NEW ZEALAND COLLEGE OF PSYCHIATRY FEDERAL COUNCIL BECOMES THE FIRST MEDICAL BODY IN THE WORLD TO DECLARE THAT HOMOSEXUALITY IS NOT AN ILLNESS.

1975

US

21 YEARS AFTER IT WAS FIRST INCLUDED, THE AMERICAN PSYCHIATRIC ASSOCIATION REMOVES HOMOSEXUALITY FROM ITS *DIAGNOSTIC AND STATISTICAL MANUAL OF MENTAL DISORDERS*.

LGBTQ+ POLITICIANS

The increasing number of LGBTQ+ people elected to political office shows that the political glass ceiling is gradually cracking open. The map below celebrates the political trailblazers.

1974 — US
Kathy Kozachenko
First openly LGBTQ+ politician to serve on a city council

1976 — THE NETHERLANDS
Coos Huijsen
First openly LGBTQ+ member of parliament

1976 — UK
Maureen Colquhoun
First openly gay female member of parliament

1979 — ITALY
Angelo Pezzana
First openly gay member of parliament

1985 — CANADA, QUEBEC
Maurice Richard
First openly gay member of the National Assembly of Quebec

1985 — GERMANY
Herbert Ludwig Rusche
First openly gay member of parliament

1987 — FINLAND
Pekka Haavisto
First openly gay member of parliament

1989 — SRI LANKA
Mangala Samaraweera
First openly gay member of parliament

1991 — SWEDEN
Kent Carlsson
First openly gay member of parliament

1992 — BRAZIL
Kátia Tapety
First transgender alderperson

1995 — SOUTH AFRICA
Edwin Cameron
First openly gay high court judge

1995 — NEW ZEALAND
Georgina Beyer
World's first openly transgender mayor (and MP, in 1999)

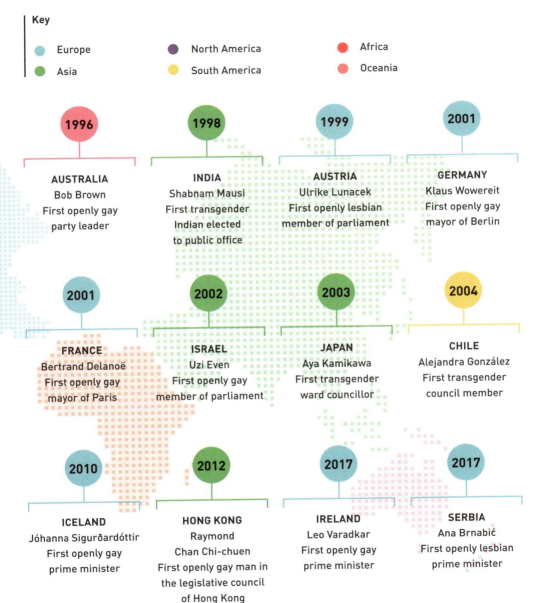

"If a bullet should enter my brain, let that bullet destroy every closet door."

Harvey Milk was an American gay rights activist and community leader who became California's first openly gay elected official in 1977. During his time as a city supervisor he worked to protect the rights of marginalized communities and sponsored an important law prohibiting discrimination based on sexual orientation. He was assassinated alongside mayor George Moscone on November 27, 1978, after just eleven months in office. For many members of the LGBTQ+ community Harvey Milk was a beacon of hope during a time of widespread discrimination. He was awarded the Presidential Medal of Freedom in 2009 and continues to be celebrated as an LGBTQ+ hero of freedom and equality.

Harvey Milk
AMERICAN
___
1930-1978

1987

UK

PRINCESS DIANA OPENS THE FIRST UK WARD DEDICATED TO HIV/AIDS TREATMENT AT LONDON'S MIDDLESEX HOSPITAL. SHE IS PHOTOGRAPHED SHAKING THE HAND OF A MAN DIAGNOSED WITH AIDS IN A TIME WHEN THE ILLNESS WAS BELIEVED TO BE TRANSMITTABLE BY TOUCH.

HIV DOES NOT MAKE PEOPLE DANGEROUS TO KNOW, SO YOU CAN SHAKE THEIR HANDS AND GIVE THEM A HUG. HEAVEN KNOWS THEY NEED IT.

DIANA, PRINCESS OF WALES (1961–1997)

1982

UK

THE DEATH OF TERRY HIGGINS, ONE OF THE EARLIEST DEATHS FROM AIDS IN BRITAIN, LEADS TO THE FOUNDATION OF THE TERRENCE HIGGINS TRUST, THE FIRST CHARITY DEDICATED TO HELPING THOSE SUFFERING FROM THE DISEASE.

1983

WEST GERMANY

A DIVERSE GROUP OF MEDICAL PROFESSIONALS AND GAY MEN FOUND DEUTSCHE AIDS-HILFE (THE NATIONAL GERMAN AIDS ORGANIZATION), WHICH DEVELOPS INTO A POWERFUL, INDEPENDENT ASSOCIATION OF AFFILIATE GROUPS ADVOCATING FOR BETTER HIV PREVENTION AND SUPPORT.

1987 — US

Larry Kramer founds ACT UP (the AIDS Coalition to Unleash Power) in New York City. It protests the slow pace of the federal drug approval, leading to new regulations to speed up drug approval. The movement grows, setting up 148 chapters in nineteen countries.

1994 — India

Anjali Gopalan founds the Naz Foundation in Delhi. It leads the legal battle against discrimination on the basis of sexual orientation and is one of the first organizations to offer care and support for individuals in India affected by HIV/AIDS.

"The dream, the only dream that any ACT UP member carries in his heart is simple: One day AIDS will be eradicated."

French writer, journalist, and LGBTQ+ activist Didier Lestrade is known for his leading role in the fight against AIDS. He worked for gay publications *Gaie Presse* and *Gai Pied* and founded the main French gay and lesbian magazine, *Têtu*. His fight against AIDS consolidated in 1989 when he cofounded the French Branch of ACT UP, acting as its president for the first three years. In 1992, Lestrade helped found TRT-5, a collective of the main French AIDS foundations, with the aim to protect the rights of people suffering from AIDS. Lestrade has published three books, including a history of ACT UP-Paris and an essay on AIDS.

Didier Lestrade
FRENCH

1958–

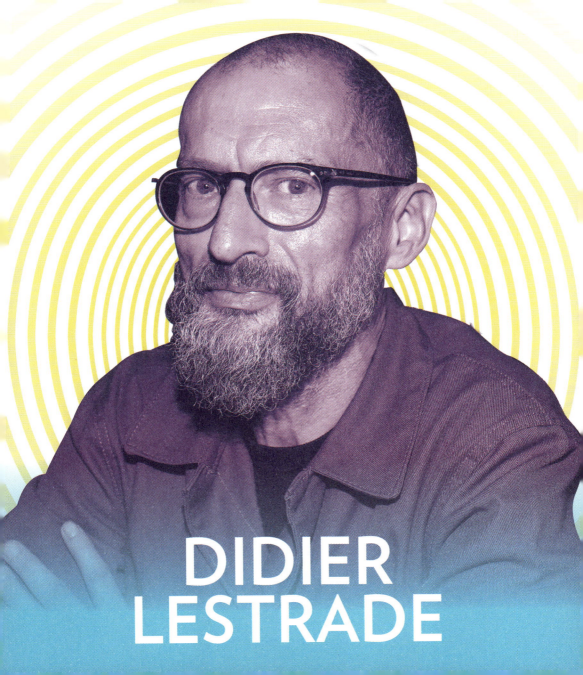

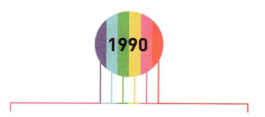

GLOBAL

1990

THE INTERNATIONAL GAY AND LESBIAN HUMAN RIGHTS COMMISSION (IGLHRC) IS FOUNDED IN NEW YORK. IT'S THE FIRST NONGOVERNMENTAL ORGANIZATION DEVOTED TO ADVANCING LGBTQ+ RIGHTS WORLDWIDE. IT IS NOW ACTIVE AS OUTRIGHT ACTION INTERNATIONAL.

1994

CANADA

CANADA GRANTS REFUGEE STATUS TO LGBTQ+ PEOPLE FEARING FOR THEIR WELL-BEING IN THEIR NATIVE COUNTRIES. IN THE SAME YEAR, FEAR OF PERSECUTION DUE TO SEXUAL ORIENTATION BECOMES GROUNDS FOR ASYLUM IN THE US.

1996

UK

P VS. S AND CORNWALL COUNTY COUNCIL FINDS THAT AN EMPLOYEE ABOUT TO UNDERGO GENDER CONFIRMATION SURGERY WAS WRONGFULLY DISMISSED. IT IS THE FIRST PIECE OF CASE LAW IN THE WORLD THAT PREVENTED DISCRIMINATION AGAINST TRANS PEOPLE IN EMPLOYMENT OR VOCATIONAL EDUCATION.

1998

ECUADOR

ECUADOR BECOMES THE FIRST COUNTRY IN THE AMERICAS (AND THE THIRD COUNTRY WORLDWIDE) TO PROTECT SEXUAL ORIENTATION IN ITS CONSTITUTION. DISCRIMINATION IS PROHIBITED IN ALL AREAS, FROM EMPLOYMENT TO THE PROVISION OF GOODS AND SERVICES.

NEW LEGAL PROTECTIONS

"Your silence will not protect you."

American writer, feminist, and civil rights activist Audre Lorde was born in New York City by Caribbean immigrants. She affirmed her identity as a lesbian and a poet while studying in Mexico, and she played a pivotal role in the gay cultural scene of Greenwich Village when she returned to New York. Lorde worked many years as a librarian before starting to teach, and being a black lesbian woman in the predominantly white and male environment of academia affected her life, work, and social activism in the 1970s and 1980s. Lorde contributed greatly to feminist theories and race studies and her poetry is an empowering and free expression of her identity as—in her own words—"black, lesbian, mother, warrior, poet."

Audre Lorde
AMERICAN

1934–1992

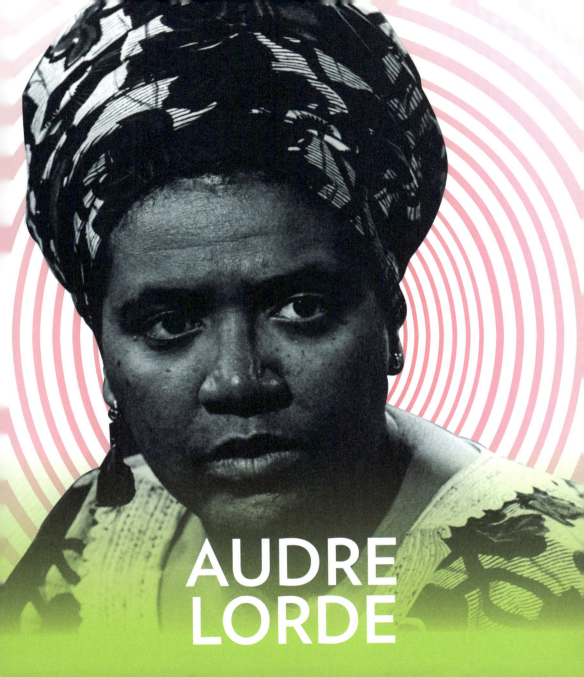

QUEER LITERATURE

LGBTQ+ stories provide wonderful insights into the experience of being lesbian, gay, bi, and trans. Not only have these works enabled the LGBTQ+ community to rally around a core of meaningful texts, they have also helped non-LGBTQ+ people to gain a better understanding of their fellow humans.

1949 Japanese author **YUKIO MISHIMA** publishes *Confessions of a Mask* in which a young man comes to terms with his sexual identity in rigid imperial Japan and is forced to hide his true feelings for his male classmate behind a mask.

1956 American Beat poet **ALLEN GINSBERG** publishes his radical poem "Howl," revolutionizing queer identity. Its violent resplendent verse gives voice to long-stifled LGBTQ+ communities in the late 1950s. It remains fresh, shocking, and entertaining.

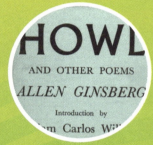

1956 **JAMES BALDWIN**, an African-American novelist, playwright, and activist, publishes what is now agreed by many to have been the greatest novel of his career—*Giovanni's Room*. In it, American protagonist David, living alone in Paris, meets Giovanni, an Italian bartender, prompting a profound exploration of homosexuality, bisexuality, and what it means to be a man.

1982 African-American author **ALICE WALKER** publishes *The Color Purple,* a novel that tackles race, gender, and sexuality within a family against the backdrop of 1930s Georgia. Although the book sparks controversy and is immediately targeted by censors, it garners critical acclaim, and Walker becomes the first black woman to win the Pulitzer Prize for Fiction.

1985 English writer **JEANETTE WINTERSON** publishes her first novel, *Oranges Are Not the Only Fruit*, a semiautobiographical story in which Jeanette, adopted by an English Pentecostal family and raised to be a missionary, realizes that she is attracted to another girl and has to leave her home and church behind.

2010 Puerto-Rican writer **LUIS NEGRÓN** publishes his debut short story collection, *Mundo Cruel*, which chronicles the lives of a queer community in the Santurce neighborhood of San Juan in Puerto Rico. The book has been reprinted five times in Spanish, and its English translation won the Lamda Literary Award for Gay Fiction in 2014.

2012 The first openly gay Moroccan writer and filmmaker **ADBELLAH TAÏA** publishes *Infidels*, a semiautobiographical novel that gains him recognition on a global scale. Violent and powerful, the book tells the brief life story of Jallal, the son of a prostitute, who grows up to become a jihadi.

2015 Nigerian-American novelist and short-story writer **CHINELO OKPARANTA** publishes her debut novel, *Under the Udala Tree*, which documents the passionate relationship between two young refugee girls displaced by the Nigerian Civil War.

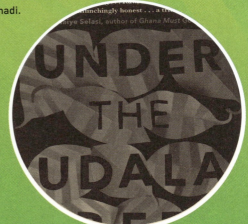

3 21st-Century Rights
2000 until today

LGBTQ+ rights enter
the mainstream agenda:
- same-sex marriage
- transgender rights
- family rights and adoption
- formal apologies to
  the LGBTQ+ community

2000 — *Dawson's Creek* shows the first gay kiss on US primetime TV

2000 — *Buffy the Vampire Slayer* shows TV's first committed lesbian relationship

2005 — *Brokeback Mountain* is released, going on to win three Academy Awards

2009 — *Modern Family* debuts on ABC, depicting a gay couple and their adopted daughter

WE'RE HERE, WE'RE QUEER

The march toward LGBTQ+ equality picked up pace during the early twenty-first century as the movement gained increased visibility and media attention. Same-sex marriage became a reality for millions of LGBTQ+ couples around the world and trans rights were put firmly on the political map.

The Netherlands led the way for other countries to follow when they legalized same-sex marriage in 2001. As of 2020, same-sex marriage is legal in thirty countries, mainly in Europe and the Americas. A ruling by the European Court of Justice in 2018 granted same-sex spouses of EU citizens the same residency rights as heterosexual spouses under the bloc's freedom-of-movement laws.

In 2012, trans rights activists in Argentina secured a landmark victory as the country passed the Gender Identity Law, granting individuals the right to define their own gender identity on official documents, without first having to receive counseling or surgery. Another cause for celebration came in 2018, when the World Health Organization (WHO) removed transgenderism from its list of mental health disorders.

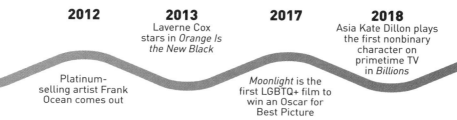

2012
Platinum-selling artist Frank Ocean comes out

2013
Laverne Cox stars in *Orange Is the New Black*

2017
Moonlight is the first LGBTQ+ film to win an Oscar for Best Picture

2018
Asia Kate Dillon plays the first nonbinary character on primetime TV in *Billions*

Progress for trans rights met with backlash in some areas, indicating the persistence of prejudice and hostile opinion. Victories for trans athletes attracted criticism from the general public and other athletes. When Canadian trans-woman cyclist Rachel McKinnon broke records, winning a track world championship title in 2018, she received more than 100,000 hate messages on social media. Despite this, trans rights continued to gain prominence, and the increasingly online world gave the trans community better visibility as well as facilitating communication and education via online activism.

The 2000s saw considerable progress in the fight for equal rights in the military. By the end of its second decade, the number of countries that allowed gays and lesbians to serve openly had risen to more than fifty from just a handful twenty years earlier. Inclusion of trans people, however, has been slower, with US President Donald Trump reinstating the ban on transgender troops in 2017. Despite this setback, the number of countries that allow transgender troops to serve openly is growing, and many are taking steps to ensure their armed forces are free from discrimination against LGBTQ+ individuals.

21ST CENTURY IN CONTEXT

The rise of the internet allowed liberation movements, including the fight for LGBTQ+ rights, to become truly global, with people across the world galvanized by communication platforms and empowered unprecedented access to education online.

2001 — 9/11 AND THE WAR ON TERROR
After the September 11 terrorist attacks on the World Trade Center and the Pentagon by Islamic terrorist group al-Qaeda, the United States government launched a "war on terror," an international military campaign aimed at radical terrorist networks. The campaign and its name have been widely criticized and President Barack Obama formally ended it in 2013.

2007/8 — GREAT RECESSION
In the years following the financial crisis of 2007/8 many parts of the world experienced a period of sustained economic decline. The IMF labeled the Great Recession the most severe economic meltdown since the 1930s and in many of the affected countries it caused political instability.

2009 — BARACK OBAMA
When Barack Obama became the USA's first black president in 2009, it was seen as evidence of the progress made since the civil rights movement of the 1960s. In his election campaign, Obama pledged to expand state health care and end US military involvement in Iraq and Afghanistan. He was awarded the Nobel Peace Prize in 2009, and during his presidency, the US government made significant progress for LGBTQ+ rights.

2010s — ARAB SPRING
The Arab Spring saw a series of protests and rebellions taking place in North Africa and the Middle East in the early 2010s, in response to oppressive regimes and low standards of living. In a region where LGBTQ+ people still suffer from discriminatory laws and persecution, many activists hoped the revolutions would usher in a new era of equality but, with the exception of Tunisia, the Arab Spring gave way to a period of instability, counter-revolution, and civil war that came to be known as the Arab Winter.

2013 — POPE FRANCIS

Elected in 2013, Pope Francis became the first pope from the Americas, and the first non-European pope for over 1,000 years. In the same year he was named gay magazine *The Advocate*'s Person of the Year for his assertion that the Catholic Church must welcome all people, regardless of sexuality. In 2016 he spoke in favor of transgender people receiving pastoral care, but his views on gender identity have been criticized. While there is still a way to go, Pope Francis has made progress for an institution that has, historically, seen homosexuality as a sin.

2016 — THE RISE OF RIGHT-WING POPULISM

In Europe and the US, the politics of the mid-2010s was dominated by the rise of the right wing. Still recovering from the Great Recession of the late 2000s, far-right politicians throughout Europe tapped into fears of mass-immigration amid the European Refugee Crisis. The 2016 Brexit vote and election of Donald Trump to the US presidency are considered part of this trend toward de-globalization and nativist stances. In Brazil and the Philippines, far-right leaders Jair Bolsonaro and Rodrigo Duterte have been criticized internationally for their discriminatory comments against LGBTQ+ people.

2017 — THE #ME TOO MOVEMENT

Tarana Burke's hashtag #metoo is popularized by American actress Alyssa Milano, encouraging women around the world to share their experiences of sexual violence. The campaign gained huge momentum, being used by more than 4.7 million on Facebook in the first twenty-four hours, and spreading to more than eighty-five countries with sister hashtags such as #YoTambien in Spain, #BalanceTonPorc in France ("expose your pig") and #quellavoltache in Italy ("that time when").

2018 — CLIMATE EMERGENCY

Climate change became a topic of international concern during the 2010s, as the effects of human-caused global warming began to be seen. Rising temperatures and an increase of natural disasters caused governments, populations, and scientists to take action. Swedish student Greta Thunberg's school strikes and powerful speeches made her a global symbol of the protest movement.

2004

FRANCE

THE MAYOR OF BÈGLES, FRANCE, CELEBRATES A HOMOSEXUAL MARRIAGE AS AN ACT OF DEFIANCE. WHILE BOTH HE AND THE COUPLE ARE SUED AND THE MARRIAGE ANNULLED, THEY SUCCEED IN RAISING THE QUESTION OF GAY MARRIAGE IN THE COUNTRY.

THE DENIAL OF GAY MARRIAGE SENDS A PREJUDICE MESSAGE. OUR YOUTH DESERVE A FAIR AND HOPEFUL FUTURE WITH GOVERNMENT THAT VALUES US EQUALLY.

LADY GAGA (1986–)
AMERICAN SINGER, ACTRESS, AND LGBTQ+ ADVOCATE

"Love is so simple and spiritual. It is not related to social status, age or even sexual identity."

Sociologist Li Yinhe played a large role in increasing public acceptance of LGBTQ+ groups in mainland China during her time at the Chinese Academy of Social Sciences. In 1992, she and her husband published the first major study into underground Chinese LGBTQ+ subcultures entitled *Their World: A Study of Homosexuality in China*. She also used her position to submit several proposals to the Chinese National Congress calling for the legalization of same-sex marriage. Since retiring from academic life in 2012, she continues to contribute to public discourse on sexual minorities through her blog, revealing that she had been in a long-term relationship with a transgender man since her husband's death.

Li Yinhe
CHINESE

1952–

SAME-SEX MARRIAGE

As of 2020, gay marriage is legal in thirty countries in the world. A further thirteen countries, mostly in Europe, allow civil unions and registered partnerships for same-sex couples, but not marriage. Three countries recognize same-sex marriages entered into elsewhere.

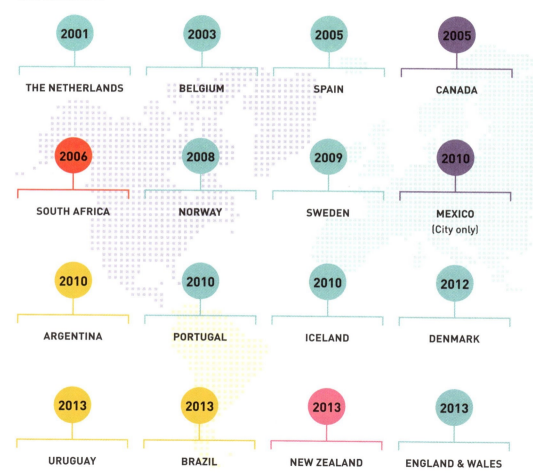

2001	2003	2005	2005
THE NETHERLANDS	BELGIUM	SPAIN	CANADA
2006	2008	2009	2010
SOUTH AFRICA	NORWAY	SWEDEN	MEXICO (City only)
2010	2010	2010	2012
ARGENTINA	PORTUGAL	ICELAND	DENMARK
2013	2013	2013	2013
URUGUAY	BRAZIL	NEW ZEALAND	ENGLAND & WALES

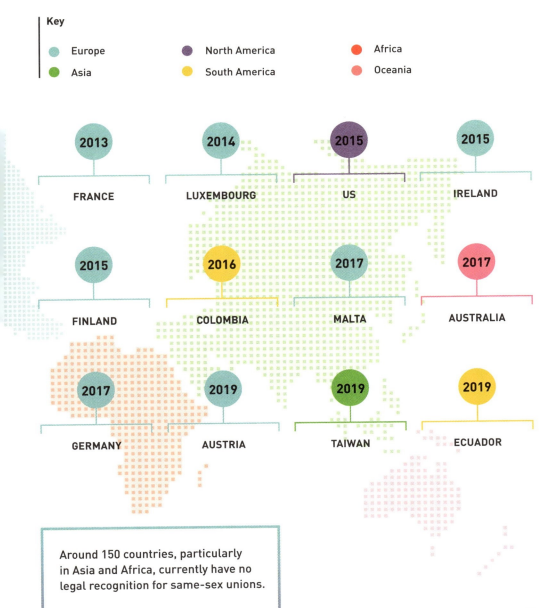

2001

THE NETHERLANDS

THE FIRST COUNTRY IN THE WORLD TO LEGALIZE SAME-SEX MARRIAGE BECOMES THE FIRST COUNTRY TO GRANT ADOPTION RIGHTS TO SAME-SEX COUPLES.

2002

SOUTH AFRICA

SUSANNE DU TOIT SUCCESSFULLY FIGHTS FOR HER PARTNER ANNA-MARIE DE VOS TO HAVE LEGAL PARENTAL RIGHTS OVER HER ADOPTIVE CHILDREN, LEADING SOUTH AFRICA TO BECOME THE FIRST AFRICAN COUNTRY TO ALLOW ADOPTION BY SAME-SEX COUPLES.

2010

FRANCE

LAWYER AND ACTIVIST CAROLINE MÉCARY WINS A TEST CASE FOR GAY PARENTS WHO HAVE CHILDREN OVERSEAS, REPRESENTING A FRENCH-AMERICAN LESBIAN COUPLE, WHERE THE FRENCH PARTNER ADOPTS THEIR CHILD CONCEIVED THROUGH ARTIFICIAL INSEMINATION IN THE US, BUT IS NOT RECOGNIZED AS THE LEGAL PARENT UNDER FRENCH LAW.

2017

US

AFTER A SUPREME COURT RULING ON JUNE 26, ADOPTION BY LGBTQ+ INDIVIDUALS OR SAME-SEX COUPLES BECOMES LEGAL IN ALL FIFTY STATES.

| LGBTQ+ COUPLES

Artists, writers and activists in history have defended the right to choose who to love through their work and in their private lives. Here are some iconic LGBTQ+ couples that proudly lived their relationships in the public eye.

1907 — American author **GERTRUDE STEIN** meets **ALICE B. TOKLAS** in Paris; their relationship starts immediately and lasts until Stein's death thirty-nine years later. The couple host a salon in their home in Paris, which becomes a meeting place for American expats and members of the Parisian avant-garde.

1922 — **VIRGINIA WOOLF** and **VITA SACKVILLE-WEST** meet for the first time, at a time when Sackville-West, ten years younger, is the more accomplished and successful writer of the two. While both women are married, their romantic relationship is facilitated by the open-minded environment of the Bloomsbury Group and supported by both husbands. Their relationship lasts ten years, eventually evolving into a long-lasting friendship.

1947 — American playwright **TENNESSEE WILLIAMS** meets and falls in love with Italian-American actor **FRANK MERLO**. The actor becomes Williams' personal secretary and the two have a long-term relationship for fourteen years. Shortly after their separation, Merlo is diagnosed with a severe form of lung cancer and Williams cares for him until his death in 1963.

1958 — French fashion designer **YVES SAINT LAURENT** meets industrialist and patron **PIERRE BERGÉ**. They begin a relationship and together launch Yves Saint Laurent Couture House in 1961, for which Bergé acts as CEO until it closes in 2002. Their romantic relationship lasts until 1976, but they remain lifelong friends and, according to *The New York Times*, were joined in a civil union (French PACS) a few days before Saint Laurent's death in 2008.

1967 Italian **GILBERT PROESCH** and English **GEORGE PASSMORE**, known as British collaborative art duo Gilbert & George, meet studying sculpture at Saint Martin's School of Art in London and begin their relationship as well as their collaboration. They enjoy decades of critical acclaim and represent the UK at the 2005 Venice Biennale. The couple marry in 2008 and live in East London.

1977 American civil and gay rights activist **BAYARD RUSTIN** meets **WALTER NAEGLE** and they start a steady relationship which lasts until Rustin's death, ten years later. Because same-sex marriage is not legal, in order to protect their relationship Rustin legally adopts Naegle in 1982. Naegle is now director of the Bayard Rustin Fund.

1994 TV personality and presenter of his eponymous *Drag Race* **RUPAUL CHARLES** meets Australian Wyoming rancher **GEORGES LEBAR** in a New York City nightclub. The two are together for an impressive twenty-three years before getting married in 2017.

2002 **CLAIRE BALDING OBE** and **ALICE ARNOLD** meet as broadcasters and journalists at the BBC and strike up a romantic relationship in 2002. They formalize their bond with a civil partnership in 2006, later marrying in a private ceremony in 2015.

2004 American comedian and TV presenter **ELLEN DEGENERES** starts dating actress and philanthropist **PORTIA DE ROSSI**. In 2008, after the overturn of the same-sex marriage ban in California, the couple marry in their home in Beverly Hills
lar couples in America.

2003

UK

THE HOMOPHOBIC LEGISLATION KNOWN AS SECTION 28 IS FINALLY REPEALED IN ENGLAND, WALES, AND NORTHERN IRELAND, LIFTING THE BAN ON LOCAL AUTHORITIES FROM "THE TEACHING IN ANY MAINTAINED SCHOOL OF THE ACCEPTABILITY OF HOMOSEXUALITY."

2011

US

CALIFORNIA STATE LEGISLATURE PASSES THE FAIR EDUCATION ACT, MAKING CALIFORNIA THE FIRST STATE IN THE US TO MANDATE THE TEACHING OF LGBTQ+ AFFIRMATIVE SOCIAL SCIENCES AND FORBIDDING DISCRIMINATORY LANGUAGE IN THE SCHOOL CURRICULUM. THE MEDIA LABELS IT THE LGBTQ+ HISTORY BILL.

2011

NEPAL

NEPAL BECOMES THE WORLD'S FIRST COUNTRY TO INCLUDE A THIRD GENDER OPTION ON ITS FEDERAL CENSUS FOR PEOPLE WHO DO NOT IDENTIFY AS MALE OR FEMALE. THIS IS DENOTED ON OFFICIAL DOCUMENTS AS "OTHER."

2015

JAPAN

THE TOKYO METROPOLITAN GOVERNMENT PASSES A BILL BANNING DISCRIMINATION ON THE BASIS OF SEXUAL ORIENTATION OR GENDER IDENTITY AND COMMITS ITSELF TO PUBLIC EDUCATION ABOUT LGBTQ+ RIGHTS.

"As long as we are living in a culture where one has to prove their womanhood or manhood, we are not living in a free culture."

Laverne Cox is an American actress, film producer, and LGBTQ+ rights activist. Her portrayal of trans people on screen as multidimensional, rather than tokenistic and stereotyped, has made her the figurehead of the world's next civil rights frontier. Not only has she given trans people more control over their own narratives through her work, but she continues to use her influence to champion trans rights on an international platform. She is also the first openly transgender person to have had a leading role in a major US television show (*Orange Is the New Black*), the first to appear on the cover of *Time* magazine, and the first to have a wax figure at Madame Tussauds.

Laverne Cox
American

1972–

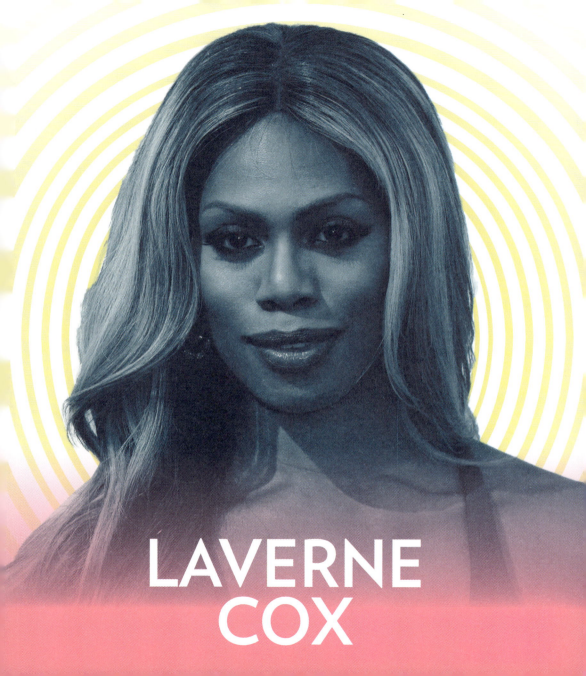

2009

US

TRANS ACTIVIST RACHEL CRANDALL FOUNDS INTERNATIONAL TRANSGENDER DAY OF VISIBILITY, ACKNOWLEDGING AND CELEBRATING LIVING MEMBERS OF THE TRANS COMMUNITY. THE EVENT IS OBSERVED ON MARCH 31.

2012

ARGENTINA

TRAILBLAZING LEGISLATION DEFINES GENDER IDENTITY AS "THE INNER AND INDIVIDUAL GENDER EXPERIENCE AS EACH PERSONS FEELS IT," RULING THAT TRANSGENDER PEOPLE ARE ABLE TO CHANGE THEIR GENDER ON GOVERNMENT DOCUMENTS WITHOUT FIRST HAVING TO RECEIVE PSYCHIATRIC COUNSELING OR TRANSITION SURGERY.

2014

INDIA

TRANSGENDER PEOPLE ARE ALLOWED TO CHANGE THEIR GENDER WITHOUT SEX REASSIGNMENT SURGERY AND HAVE THE CONSTITUTIONAL RIGHT TO REGISTER THEMSELVES UNDER A THIRD GENDER.

2017

DENMARK

DENMARK IS THE FIRST COUNTRY IN THE WORLD TO OFFICIALLY REMOVE TRANSGENDER IDENTITIES FROM ITS LIST OF MENTAL HEALTH DISORDERS. THE PARLIAMENTARY HEALTH COMMITTEE ANNOUNCES, "IT IS COMPLETELY INAPPROPRIATE TO CALL IT A SICKNESS."

LEGAL RECOGNITION FOR TRANSGENDER PEOPLE

Around a third of all countries recognize the right to legally change gender. Only six countries allow legal gender change through self-identification, with the others requiring either surgery or a medical diagnosis.

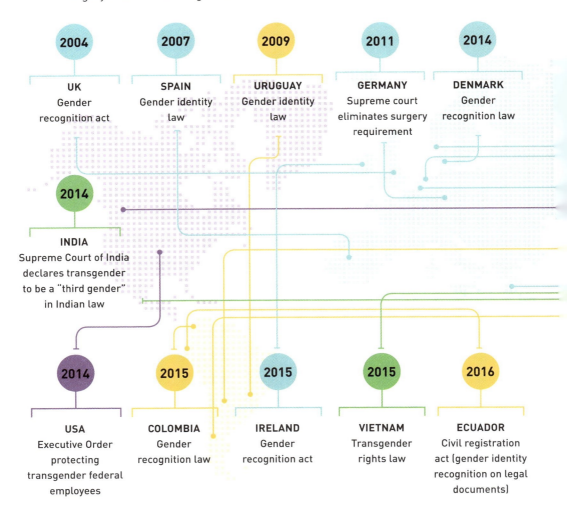

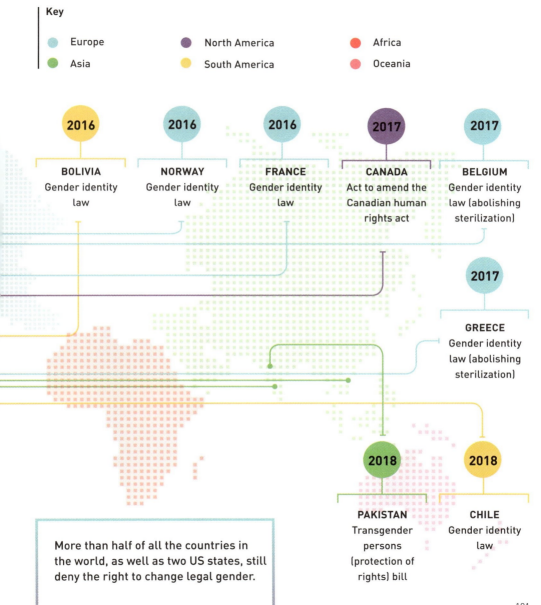

"The more people that...feel happy they can come out and know that it's not going to affect their job or moving up in their career is the way forward."

Two-time Olympic flyweight champion Nicola Adams was the first openly LGBTQ+ person to win an Olympic gold medal in boxing. Born in Leeds in 1982, she first became the English amateur champion in 2003, holding on to the title for four years in a row. Despite speaking out on the problematic nature of labels and not wanting to be defined by her sexuality, as an open bisexual, her rise to fame in sports made her an inspiration in the LGBTQ+ community. In the 2012 London Games she became the first British woman to triumph in any Olympic boxing category, and *The Independent* named her "the most influential LGBT individual in Britain." She became world champion the same year and defended her Olympic title in Rio de Janeiro four years later. She retired in 2019, unbeaten as a professional boxer.

Nicola Adams
BRITISH

1982–

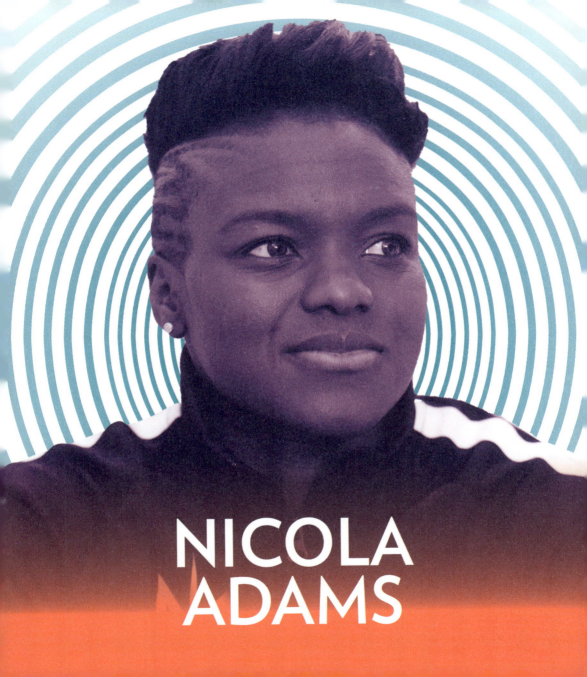

LGBTQ+ PEOPLE IN SPORTS

While the stigma against being openly LGBTQ+ in professional sports still persists (especially for men in team sports like football), several LGBTQ+ identifying sportspeople have managed to rise to the top of their sport. These figures have been inspirational to both queer and non-LGBTQ+ youths and have helped to normalize queer identity in wider culture.

1981 — American **BILLIE JEAN KING** becomes the first prominent sportsperson to come out as a lesbian. A former world number one ranked tennis player, she won thirty-nine Grand Slam titles before retiring in 1983. She is widely regarded as one of the greatest tennis players in the history of the sport and was an influential pioneer in pushing for gender equality in tennis.

1990 — Shortly after leaving professional team Leyton Orient, **JUSTIN FASHANU** becomes the first English soccer player to publicly come out as gay. He subsequently kills himself eight years later after being accused of sexually assaulting a boy in Maryland, where homosexual acts were illegal at the time.

1995 — Arguably the greatest athlete in diving history, four-time Olympic gold medal winner American **GREG LOUGANIS** becomes one of the most high profile sports stars to admit they are HIV positive. He had publicly come out as gay during the Gay Games a year earlier.

1999 — Transgender Thai kickboxing champion **PARINYA CHAROENPHOL**, who fought under the name Nong Toom, uses the money she earned from her bouts to pay for sex reassignment surgery.

2009 — **GARETH THOMAS**, then Wales's most capped rugby union player, becomes the first professional sportsman in a team sport to come out of the closet while playing for a professional team.

2010 — Two-time FIFA World Cup winner **NADINE ANGERER** discloses her bisexuality to a German newspaper. She is one of the most decorated women soccer players, having also won five European Championships with Germany and being named the best women's player in the world in 2013.

2013 — Former NFL player **KWAME HARRIS** comes out as gay. The Jamaican-born football player describes himself as having to "worry about maintaining this mask" as a closeted man in the sport.

2014 — Australian swimmer **IAN THORPE** comes out as gay on television. He is the most successful Australian at the Olympics, having won five gold medals in 2000 and 2004.

2015 — **CAITLYN JENNER**, who won a gold medal in the decathlon at the 1976 Olympics, publicly comes out as a transgender woman, beginning her transitioning before having sex reassignment surgery in 2017. A controversial figure within the LGBTQ+ community, she is arguably the most high profile transgender woman in the world.

2019 — **MEGAN RAPINOE** is named the best women's soccer player in the world. A prominent figure within the LGBTQ+ community, Rapinoe plays a key role in helping the USA with the World Cup in the same year, winning the award for player of the tournament as well as top scorer.

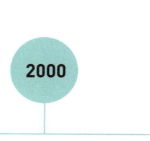

2000

GERMANY

THE BUNDESWEHR (THE GERMAN ARMY) RULES THAT SEXUAL ORIENTATION IS NO LONGER A VALID REASON TO PREVENT SOMEONE FROM SERVING IN A COMMANDING ROLE.

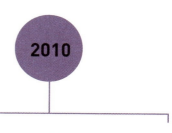

2010

USA

THE US ARMY'S CONTROVERSIAL "DON'T ASK, DON'T TELL" POLICY, WHICH PREVENTED LGBTQ+ PERSONNEL FROM SERVING OPENLY, IS REPEALED. SINCE ITS IMPLEMENTATION IN 1993, IT HAD LED TO 13,000 DISCHARGES.

2011

THE NETHERLANDS

THE DUTCH ARMED FORCES PARTICIPATE IN AMSTERDAM PRIDE FOR THE FIRST TIME WITH THEIR OWN "DEFENCE BOAT." THE NETHERLANDS WAS ALSO THE FIRST COUNTRY TO LIFT ITS BAN ON HOMOSEXUALS SERVING IN THE MILITARY.

2012

NEW ZEALAND

THE NEW ZEALAND DEFENCE FORCE ESTABLISHES OVERWATCH, AN LGBTQ+ SUPPORT GROUP DESIGNED TO INCREASE INCLUSIVITY AND REMOVE DISCRIMINATION. IT HAS LEAD TO THE COUNTRY'S MILITARY BECOMING ONE OF THE MOST INCLUSIVE IN THE WORLD.

"'Don't Ask, Don't Tell' says you have to lie. It forces people to lie, to hide. Hiding and lying aren't army values."

When US Army Lieutenant Dan Choi came out as gay on national television in March 2009, he was bravely challenging his employer's infamous mantra of "Don't Ask, Don't Tell." The policy, which had been in place since 1994, forbade openly queer identifying individuals from serving in the American armed forces. Choi's subsequent discharge drew widespread condemnation and made him a prominent figure in the American gay community, being chosen as Grand Marshal of the 41st New York Pride March in 2010. That same year he was arrested three times for chaining himself to the White House in protest against his dismissal and "Don't Ask, Don't Tell." His courage led to a judgment ruling that the policy was unconstitutional, and it was repealed by President Obama.

Dan Choi

American

1981–

LGBTQ+ IN THE MILITARY

It is legal in around fifty countries for some LGBTQ+ identifying individuals to serve openly in the military. In most countries, the laws were initially only changed to allow gay and lesbian people to serve. As of 2020, nineteen countries allow transgender people to serve in their armed forces.

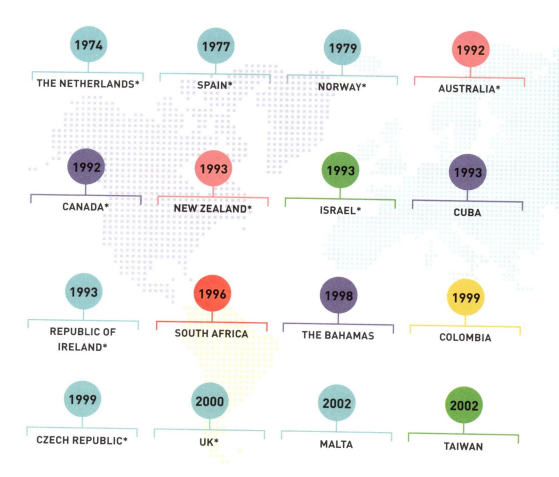

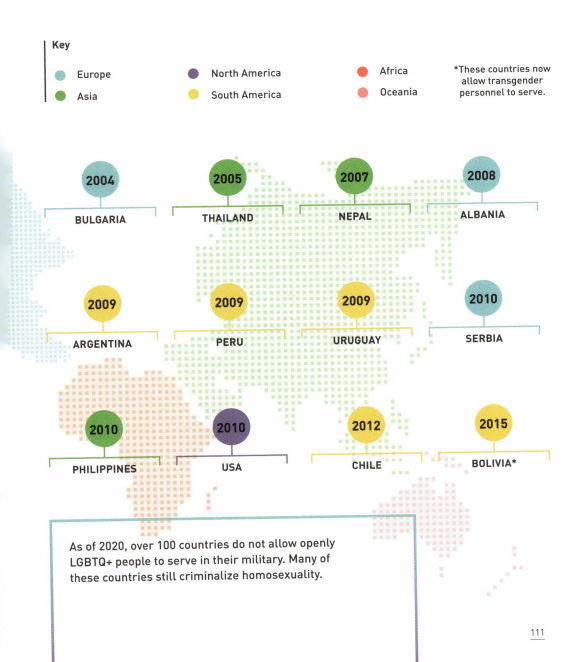

LGBTQ+ ACTIVISM ONLINE

The internet has revolutionized how LGBTQ+ activists organize. In particular, social media platforms have facilitated growing solidarity, enabling the growth of international online communities and protest movements via Twitter, Facebook, and Instagram.

1987 — One of the first email discussion lists for lesbian and bisexual women, **SAPPHO**, is founded by Jean Marie Diaz. It soon becomes well known and spawns several smaller lists that constitute a safe space to discuss matters of interest to the lesbian community such as coming out, safe sex, and online dating.

1992 — **THE KHUSH LIST** is established: a completely confidential mailing list and online discussion space for South Asian people who identify as LGBTQ+. Its purpose is to discuss South Asian gay culture, experiences, and issues, as well as to form a social and support network for the subscribers.

1995 — Founded by Tom Rielly in 1995, and still one of the main global media companies specifically aimed at the LGBTQ+ demographic, **PLANETOUT** is launched on the Microsoft Network and operates several LGBTQ+-themed websites. In 2000 it merges with its biggest competitor, Gay.com, becoming PlanetOut Partners, Inc.

1999 — **TRANSGENDER DAY OF REMEMBRANCE (TDoR)**
TDoR is founded as a web-based project by Gwendolyn Ann Smith to memorialize the murder of transgender woman Rita Hester. It is now a day observed internationally every November 20, to draw attention to the violence and transphobia transgender people have to face.

2007 — **TUMBLR** is founded and becomes a hub for LGBTQ+ youth from around the world, bringing formerly fringe movements into the mainstream and providing a safe space for queer people to explore their identity.

2010 — Gay activists Dan Savage and Terry Miller launch the **IT GETS BETTER** project on YouTube with the aim of preventing suicides among LGBTQ+ youth by having gay adults communicate to them that their lives will get better. More than 200 videos are uploaded in the first week. Today, the platform has its own website and has amassed over fifty million views.

2013 — Millions of Facebook users change their profile picture to a pink and red version of The Human Rights Campaign's equality logo to show their support for gay marriage.

2014 — Despite harsh laws criminalising homosexuality, Ugandan LGBTQ+ activists launch the online ***BOMBASTIC MAGAZINE***, documenting LGBTQ+ life in the country and advocating legal reform.

2015 — After the Supreme Court rules that gay marriage is legal in all fifty states, the hashtag **#lovewins** is used over 5.5 million times on Twitter in the US, including in a tweet by President Barack Obama. Facebook creates a filter to superimpose a rainbow banner over the profile picture. The filter is used by millions of people, including Facebook founder Mark Zuckerberg.

2016 — The pro-LGBTQ+ rights collective **ASWAT** uses the hashtag **#loveisnotacrime** to draw international attention to violence against LGBTQ+ people in Morocco.

2017 — Trans activists in Turkey successfully organise a trans street parade on the streets of Istanbul using the hashtag **#gameoftrans** across several social media platforms.

"The day is not far when discrimination against people based on who they love will also be left behind in the wastebasket of history."

One of the most outspoken human rights activists in Africa, Kasha Jacqueline Nabagesera has campaigned for LGBTQ+ rights since 2002, when she was almost expelled from university because of her sexuality. She founded Freedom and Roam Uganda (FARUG) in 2003, serving as its executive director for ten years and fighting for the protection of LGBTQ+ people and the decriminalization of homosexuality in Africa. She later founded *Kunchu Times*, which uses the media to broadcast LGBTQ+ news, and *Bombastic Magazine*, which shares the stories of the Ugandan LGBTQ+ community. Today, she appeals on a global platform to advocate for LGBTQ+ rights in Africa—tirelessly fighting for her cause against incredible odds at the United Nations, the African Commission, and the European Union.

Kasha Nabagesera
Ugandan

1980–

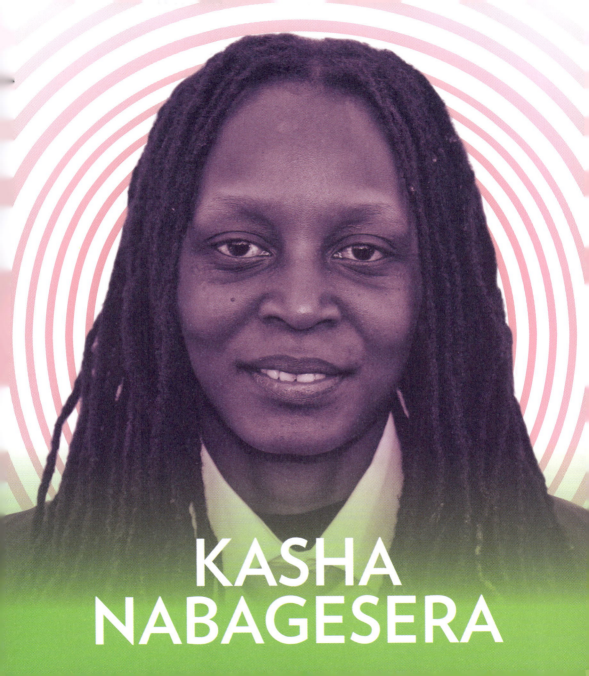

2007 — SPAIN

AS PART OF THE LANDMARK LAW OF HISTORICAL MEMORY, IT BECOMES POSSIBLE FOR ANYONE WHO SUFFERED ECONOMIC HARDSHIP BECAUSE OF THEIR SEXUAL ORIENTATION TO SEEK COMPENSATION FROM THE STATE.

2009 — UK

CONSERVATIVE PARTY LEADER AND FUTURE PRIME MINISTER DAVID CAMERON OFFERS A HISTORIC PUBLIC APOLOGY FOR MARGARET THATCHER'S SECTION 28, THE LEGISLATION THAT BANNED THE "PROMOTION" OF HOMOSEXUALITY IN SCHOOLS.

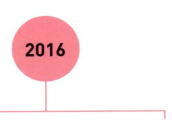

2016

AUSTRALIA

FORMAL APOLOGY BY NEW SOUTH WALES POLICE FORCE FOR THEIR BRUTAL TREATMENT OF LGBTQ+ ACTIVISTS IN THE MARDI GRAS DEMONSTRATION IN JUNE 1978. MEMBERS OF PARLIAMENT ALSO MAKE APOLOGIES ON BEHALF OF THE STATE GOVERNMENT.

2017

CANADA

PRIME MINISTER TRUDEAU DELIVERS A HISTORIC APOLOGY TO LGBTQ+ CANADIANS IN THE HOUSE OF COMMONS FOR DECADES OF "STATE-SPONSORED, SYSTEMATIC OPPRESSION AND REJECTION."

2018

UK

IN RESPONSE TO A CAMPAIGN LED BY ACTIVIST PETER TATCHELL, THERESA MAY APOLOGIZES FOR BRITAIN'S LEGACY OF ANTIGAY LAWS AND URGES COMMONWEALTH NATIONS TO OVERHAUL COLONIAL-ERA LEGISLATION THAT TREATS OVER 100 MILLION LGBTQ+ PEOPLE ACROSS THE MEMBER COUNTRIES AS CRIMINALS.

2019

US

THE AMERICAN PSYCHOANALYTIC ASSOCIATION OFFER A PUBLIC APOLOGY FOR HISTORICALLY LABELLING HOMOSEXUALITY AS A MENTAL ILLNESS, EXTENDING A HISTORIC RECOGNITION OF THE ROLE THIS LABEL PLAYED IN THE ONGOING DISCRIMINATION AGAINST LGBTQ+ PEOPLE.

ALL OF US WHO ARE OPENLY GAY ARE LIVING AND WRITING THE HISTORY OF OUR MOVEMENT.

SENATOR TAMMY BALDWIN
UNITED STATES SENATOR, AND THE FIRST OPENLY GAY WOMAN ELECTED TO THE UNITED STATES CONGRESS

QUEER FILM

Film has always served as an important medium for capturing queer experience, challenging heteronormativity, and increasing the visibility of LGBTQ+ lives. This list is a very short selection of the classic on-screen portrayals of LGBTQ+ life.

1950 — *Un Chant d'Amour*, the only film directed by French writer **JEAN GENET**, is released. The erotic twenty-six-minute short is set in a French prison and follows the voyeuristic gaze of a guard who watches the inmates masturbate. It is banned for many years because of the homosexual relationships explored in the film.

1961 — English film director **BASIL DEARDEN**'s groundbreaking thriller *Victim* is released. Many people believe the film plays an influential role in the decriminalization of homosexuality in the UK. In it, Dirk Bogarde plays a successful barrister coming to terms with his sexuality while being blackmailed by people who threaten to expose photos of him with another man.

1968 — Japanese Drag artist **AKIHIRO MIWA** plays the leading role of a female jewel thief in *Black Lizard*. His close friend Yukio Mishima writes the screenplay, adapting it from an earlier novel and writing the part especially for Miwa.

1972 — German filmmaker **RAINER WERNER FASSBINDER** directs an all-female cast in *The Bitter Tears of Petra von Kant*, which follows a narcissistic fashion designer's relationships with the women she employs. It is a meditation on obsession, power, solitude, and destructive affairs.

1997 — Chinese director **WONG KAR-WAI**'s *Happy Together* is released. This portrayal of two gay men on holiday in Argentina becomes a classic of gay cinema, and wins Kar-wai the award for Best Director at the 1997 Cannes Film Festival. It charts the turbulent journey of a failing relationship with a powerful intimacy.

2004 | Thai filmmaker **APICHATPONG WEERASETHAKUL** releases *Tropical Malady*, a psychological drama that tells two stories: a love story about a soldier and a country boy, and then the surreal tale of a soldier who is lost in the woods and tormented by a shaman. It wins the Jury Prize at Cannes in 2004, and is the first Thai film to be in the main competition.

2005 | Taiwanese filmmaker **ANG LEE** releases *Brokeback Mountain*, a romantic drama in which Heath Ledger and Jake Gyllenhaal star as isolated sheepherders in Wyoming who fall in love and experience heartbreak and regret for the rest of their lives. It is a lyrical and reflective work and is, deservedly, a landmark moment in cinema.

2013 | French-Tunisian actor and director **ABDELLATIF KECHICHE** wins the Palme d'Or at Cannes for his film *Blue is the Warmest Color*. This sensational coming-of-age story follows the lives of fifteen-year-old Adèle and the mesmeric art student Emma and the complex love affair between them. Upon its release, the film generates much controversy after Léa Seydoux and Adèle Exarchopoulos, the two leading actors, complain about Kechiche's behavior on set, describing it as "horrible."

2016 | American filmmaker **BARRY JENKINS** releases *Moonlight*, a groundbreaking and heartrending portrayal of black gay masculinity in the US. Jenkins's Bildungsroman is set in poverty-stricken Miami, and follows the life of Chiron on his troubled journey to self-realization. A vital portrait of black queer culture, *Moonlight* is the first LGBTQ+ film—and the first film with an all-black cast—to win the Oscar for Best Picture. It also wins the Academy Award for Best Supporting Actor and the Golden Globe for Best Motion Picture—Drama, among several other awards.

2017 | *A Fantastic Woman* is released. Directed by **SEBASTIÁN LELIO**, this Chilean drama centers on transgender singer and waitress Marina. Starring transgender actress Daniela Vega, the film illustrates the complications and transphobia she has to face from the authorities and her partner's family after his accidental death. The film wins the Academy Award for Best Foreign Language Film in 2017.

A GUIDE TO LGBTQ+ FLAGS

Symbols, flags, and other forms of insignia have played an important role in the history of the LGBTQ+ rights movement, helping to build solidarity for members of the queer community. A selection of some of the most common are included below, with notes on their origins and history.

LGBTQ+ PRIDE FLAG
Instantly recognizable, the rainbow Pride flag was designed by Gilbert Baker in 1978 for the San Francisco Gay Freedom Day celebration. The rainbow is a symbol of diversity: In the original eight-color version, pink stood for sexuality, red for life, orange for healing, yellow for sunlight, green for nature, turquoise represented art, indigo symbolized harmony and violet, spirit. The flag most associated with LGBTQ+ pride today has only six colors, having lost the pink and turquoise.

BISEXUAL PRIDE FLAG
Designing this flag to foster a sense of solidarity in the bisexual community in 1998, Michael Page chose pink to represent sexual attraction to the same sex only, blue to represent attraction to the opposite sex and lavender to symbolize attraction to both sexes (or anywhere along the gender spectrum). As such, the flag references queerness and brings visibility to the Bs of LGBTQ+ within society as a whole and the LGBTQ+ community.

TRANSGENDER PRIDE FLAG
The transgender Pride flag was designed by American trans woman Monica Helms in 1999. The light blue is the traditional color for baby boys and the pink for girls. The white in the middle is for those who are transitioning, those who feel they have a neutral gender or no gender, and those who are intersex. Helms said on designing the flag: "No matter which way you fly it, it will always be correct. This symbolizes us trying to find correctness in our own lives."

INTERSEX PRIDE FLAG
Designed in 2013 by Intersex International Australia, the intersex Pride flag uses non-gendered colors to celebrate living outside the binary.

PANSEXUAL PRIDE FLAG

The pansexual Pride flag was designed by Evie Varney in 2010 as a means of bringing visibility to the pansexual community. The pink and blue stripes on either side of the central gold stripe respectively symbolize female and male gendered persons (regardless of biological sex), while the gold identifies those of a mixed gender, a third gender, or those who are genderless.

GENDERQUEER FLAG

Marilyn Roxie first designed the genderqueer flag in 2010. The separate colors, Roxie emphasized, "are not meant to indicate that any of these identities are entirely separate or opposites of one another conceptually." The lavender represents androgyny, the white represents agender identity, and the green represents those whose identities are defined outside of and without reference to the gender binary.

ASEXUAL PRIDE FLAG

According to the Asexuality Archive, this flag was created by a member of the Asexual Visibility and Education Network (AVEN) as part of a contest in 2010. The black stripe stands for asexuality, the gray stripe for gray asexuality or demisexuality, the white for allies, and the purple for the asexual community as a whole.

PROGRESS FLAG

In 2018, designer Daniel Quasar began a campaign to "reboot" the Pride flag to make it more inclusive by adding a five-colored chevron to represent queer people of color as well as the trans community.

GLOSSARY

AGENDER
A person who identifies as being without any gender.

ANDROGYNY
The combination of typically masculine and feminine characteristics and aesthetics into an ambiguous form, presented through outward appearance and fashion.

ASEXUAL (ACE)
Being without sexual feelings and thus sexually attracted to no one. Some "ace" people may still have sex, based on emotional rather then sexual attraction, while others are sex-averse. A common misconception is that asexual people are also aromantic, but some experience romantic attraction and form romantic relationships.

BISEXUAL (BI)
Having a sexual or romantic orientation toward more than one gender.

CISGENDER (CIS)
A person whose gender identity is the same as the sex they were assigned at birth.

COMING OUT
Revealing for the first time one's identity as LBGTQ+.

DEADNAMING
Using someone's birth name even after it has been changed (often related to change of names during and after a transition).

GAY
A man whose sexual or romantic orientation is toward men. Also the preferred term of some women instead of "lesbian."

GENDER
Cultural and behavioral traits normally associated with the sex assigned at birth in terms of femininity and masculinity.

GENDER DYSPHORIA
Discomfort caused by a mismatch between a person's gender identity and the sex assigned to them at birth.

GENDERFLUID
Relating to a person who does not identify as having a fixed gender, preferring to fluctuate between or express multiple genders simultaneously.

GENDER IDENTITY
Sense of one's gender, not necessarily corresponding to the sex assigned at birth nor necessarily corresponding to the male/female binary.

GENDER-NEUTRAL
Being suitable for or applicable to both male and female genders and thus not being exclusionary toward one or the other.

GENDER REASSIGNMENT
A transition, sometimes involving medical intervention, indicated by changes in name, pronouns, and other aspects that allow a person to live in their self-identified gender.

HETEROSEXUAL
A man whose sexual or romantic orientation is toward women or a woman whose sexual or romantic orientation is toward men. The word "straight" is also used.

HOMOPHOBIA
Fear, aversion, or discrimination against homosexuality and bisexuality.

HOMOSEXUAL
Someone whose romantic or sexual orientation is toward a person of the same gender.

INTERSEX
A person who is born with the biological attributes of both sexes, meaning that they have a variation of sex characteristics that do not fit the typical definitions for male/female bodies.

LESBIAN
A woman whose sexual or romantic orientation is toward women.

NONBINARY
Someone not identifying fully with either the male or female category, viewed as binary opposites.

ORIENTATION
A person's sexual or romantic attraction to other people.

OUTED
The disclosure of someone's orientation or gender identity without the person's consent.

PANSEXUAL (PAN)
Romantic or sexual attraction not limited by sex or gender, meaning that they can be sexually attracted to anyone regardless of sex or gender identity.

QUEER
A nonspecific term used to reject specific labels of sexual and romantic orientation as well as gender identity.

SEX
Assigned to a person at birth based on their reproductive organs and primary sex characteristics, according to the typical definitions of male and female biology.

SEXUAL ORIENTATION
Sexual attraction toward other people that forms orientation identity.

TRANSGENDER (TRANS)
Someone whose gender identity is not the same as the sex they were assigned at birth.

TRANSGENDER MAN/WOMAN
Someone who identifies as the opposite gender to that assigned to them at birth.

TRANSITIONING
The process a trans person may undergo to live in the gender with which they identify, specific to each individual and the steps that they take to achieve this.

TRANSPHOBIA
Fear of, aversion to or discrimination against someone who identifies as trans, including deadnaming and the refusal to accept their transition or gender identity.

TRANSSEXUAL
A more medical term to describe a transgender person who has had medical assistance to transition from one sex to the other, meaning that their gender is not the same as the sex assigned to them at birth.

RESOURCES

US

USC University of Southern California
usc.edu
ONE National Gay & Lesbian Archives at the USC Libraries is the largest repository of Lesbian, Gay, Bisexual, Transgender, Queer (LGBTQ) materials in the world.

Centerlink
lgbtcenters.org
The community of LGBT centers.

COLAGE
colage.org
3815 S. Othello Street, Suite 100, #310
Seattle, WA 98118
COLAGE unites people with lesbian, gay, bisexual, transgender, and/or queer parents into a network of peers and supports them as they nurture and empower each other to be skilled, self-confident, and just leaders in our collective communities.

Equality Federation
equalityfederation.org
Equality Federation is a social justice and advocacy movement supporting each stated LGBT communities.

GLAAD
glaad.org
A dynamic media force, GLAAD tackles tough issues to shape the narrative and provoke dialogue that leads to cultural change.

GLSEN
glsen.org
GLSEN's mission is to ensure that every member of every school community is valued and respected regardless of sexual orientation, gender identity, or gender expression.

Matthew Shepard Foundation
matthewshepard.org
Empowering individuals through local, regional, and national outreach to erase hate by replacing it with understanding, compassion, and acceptance.

National Center for Transgender Equality
transequality.org
The National Center for Transgender Equality advocates to change policies and society to increase understanding and acceptance of transgender people. In the nation's capital and throughout the country, NCTE works to replace disrespect, discrimination, and violence with empathy, opportunity, and justice.

The National LGBTQ Task Force
thetaskforce.org
The National LGBTQ Task Force advances full freedom, justice, and equality for LGBTQ people.

IGLYO
iglyo.com
IGLYO is a youth development and leadership organization building LGBTQI youth activists, ensuring LGBTQI young people are present and heard, and making schools safe, inclusive, and supportive of LGBTQI learners.

GSA Network
gsanetwork.org
GSA Network is a next-generation LGBTQ racial and gender justice organization that empowers and trains queer, trans, and allied youth leaders to advocate, organize, and mobilize an intersectional movement for safer schools and healthier communities.

It Gets Better Project
itgetsbetter.org
The It Gets Better Project is a non-profit organization with a mission to uplift, empower, and connect lesbian, gay, bisexual, transgender, and queer youth around the globe.

The Trevor Project
thetrevorproject.org
Founded in 1998 by the creators of the Academy Award-winning short film *Trevor*, The Trevor Project is the leading national organization providing crisis intervention and suicide prevention services to lesbian, gay, bisexual, transgender, queer, and questioning (LGBTQ) young people under 25.

CANADA

OK2BME
ok2bme.ca
KW Counselling Services
480 Charles St. East
Kitchener, ON
N2G 4K5
The OK2BME project is operated by KW Counselling Services. OK2BME is a set of free, confidential services including counselling and a youth group for kids and teens wondering about their sexuality or gender identity. They may identify as lesbian, gay, bisexual, transgender, gender-variant, or they may just have questions.

PFLAG Canada
pflagcanada.ca
Canada's LGBTQ2+ Archive. ArQuives collects and maintains collections related to LGBTQ2+ life in Canada, including books, archival papers, artifacts, photographs, and art. Founded in 1973, they have grown to become the largest independent LGBTQ2+ archive in the world.

The ArQuives, Canada's LGBTQ2+ Archives
arquives.ca
34 Isabella Street
Toronto, ON
M4Y 1N1
The ArQuives aspires to be a significant resource and catalyst for those who strive for a future world where lesbian, gay, bisexual, and trans people are accepted, valued, and celebrated.

LGBTQ+ PEOPLE FEATURED

A
Adams, Nicola 102
Angerer, Nadine 104
Arnold, Alice 93
Axgil, Axel 22, 24

B
Bacon, Francis 42
Baker, Gilbert 122
Balding, Claire 93
Baldwin Tammy, 119
Baldwin, James 76, 17
Baudry, André 22
Bergé, Pierre 92
Boswell, Holly 6
Bowery, Leigh 43
Bowie, David 48
Brand, Adolf 32
Brnabić, Ana 63
Butler, Judith 54

C
Charles, RuPaul 93
Charoenphol, Parinya 104
Choi, Dan 108
Cox, Laverne 81, 96, 97
Crandall, Rachel 98

D
De Rossi, Portia 93
Dearden, Basil 120
DeGeneres, Ellen 93, 47
Delanoë, Bertrand 63
Dillon, Asia Kate 81
Du Toit, Susanne 90

E
Edelman, Lee 55
Elagabalus 11
Elbe, Lili 12
Esteban Muñoz, José 55

F
Fashanu, Justin 104
Forster, Jakie 30,31
Foucault, Michel 33, 54

G
Gaga, Lady 85
Genet, Jean 120
Ginsberg, Allen 76
Gittings, Barbara 27, 33

H
Halberstam, Jack 55
Hang, Ren Hang 43
Hanscombe, Gill 30
Haring, Keith 42
Harris, Kwame 104
Hay, Harry 23
Helms, Monica 122
Hennessy, Rosemary 55
Hester, Rita 112
Higgins, Terry 68
Highsmith, Patricia 16
Hirshfeld, Magnus 12, 13
Höch, Hannah 42
Hockney, David 33, 42
Howard, Brenda 58
Huijsen, Coos 62

J
Jean King, Billie 104
Jenner, Caitlyn 104
John, Elton 48
Johnson, Marsha P. 36, 46
Jorgensen, Christine 16

K
Kameny, Frank 16
Kar-wai, Wong 120
Kechiche, Abdellatif 121
Kinsey, Alfred 20
Klimmer, Rudolf 26
Kosofsky Sedgwick, Eve 54
Kramer, Larry 69

L
LeBar, Georges 93
Lee, Ang 121
Lelio, Sebastián 121
Lestrade, Didier 70
Lorde, Audre 74
Louganis, Greg 104

M
Marie Diaz, Jean 112
McKinnon, Rachel 81
Mécary, Caroline 91
Merlo, Frank 92
Milk, Harvey 64, 65
Miller, Terry 113
Mishima, Yukio 32, 76, 120
Miwa, Akihiro 120
Muholi, Zanele 43

N
Nabagesera, Kasha 114
Naegle, Walter 93
Negrón, Luis 77
Nuwas, Abu 12

O
Ocean, Frank 81
Okparanta, Chinelo 77

P
Page, Michael 122
Passmore, George 93
Proesch, Gilbert 93

Q
Quasar, Daniel 123

R
Rapinoe, Megan 104
Rielly, Tom 112
Rivera, Sylvia 36, 39, 46
Rodwell, Craig 17
Roxie, Marilyn 123
Rustin, Bayard 93

S
Sackville-West, Vita 92
Saint Laurent, Yves 92
Sartre, Jean-Paul 33
Savage, Dan 113
Shikhandi 12
Sigurðardóttir, Jóhanna 63
Smith, Gwendolyn Ann 112
Stein, Gertrude 92

T
Taïa, Adbellah 77
Tapety, Kátia 62
Tatchell, Peter 47, 52, 118
Thomas, Gareth 104
Thorpe, Ian 104
Toklas, Alice B. 92

V
Varadkar, Leo 63
Varney, Evie 122

W
Wagner, Vivian 6
Walker, Alice 76
Weerasethakul, Apichatpong 121
Wiley, Kehinde 43
Williams, Tennessee 92
Winterson, Jeanette 77
Woolf, Virginia 92
Wright, Billy 16

Y
Yinhe, Li 86

An Imprint of Simon & Schuster, Inc.
1230 Avenue of the Americas
New York, NY 10020

Copyright © 2020 by Elwin Street Productions Limited

Conceived and produced by
Elwin Street Productions Limited
10 Elwin Street
London E2 7BU

All rights reserved, including the right to reproduce this book or portions thereof in any form whatsoever. For information, address Simon & Schuster Subsidiary Rights Department, 1230 Avenue of the Americas, New York, NY 10020.

First Tiller Press hardcover edition for North America May 2020

TILLER PRESS and colophon are trademarks of Simon & Schuster, Inc.

For information about special discounts for bulk purchases, please contact Simon & Schuster Special Sales at 1-866-506-1949 or business@simonandschuster.com.

The Simon & Schuster Speakers Bureau can bring authors to your live event. For more information or to book an event, contact the Simon & Schuster Speakers Bureau at 1-866-248-3049 or visit our website at www.simonspeakers.com.

Cover and interior illustrations by Rebecca Strickson © (14, 44, 78)
Interior design by Natalie Clay
Research by Rebecca Fitzsimons, Anna Gatteschi, Gage Kumar Rull, Jessica Payn, Thomas Webster

Additional picture credits:
© Getty Images: 13, 25, 31, 53, 71, 87, 103, 109; © Alamy Stock Photo: 37, 63, 75, 97, 115; Efrain John Gonzalez, Hellfirepress.com: 57; © Shutterstock, 28–29, 40–41, 56–57, 62–63, 88–89, 100–01, 110–11.

Manufactured in Malaysia

10 9 8 7 6 5 4 3 2

Library of Congress Cataloging-in-Publication Data has been applied for.

ISBN 978-1-9821-4237-7